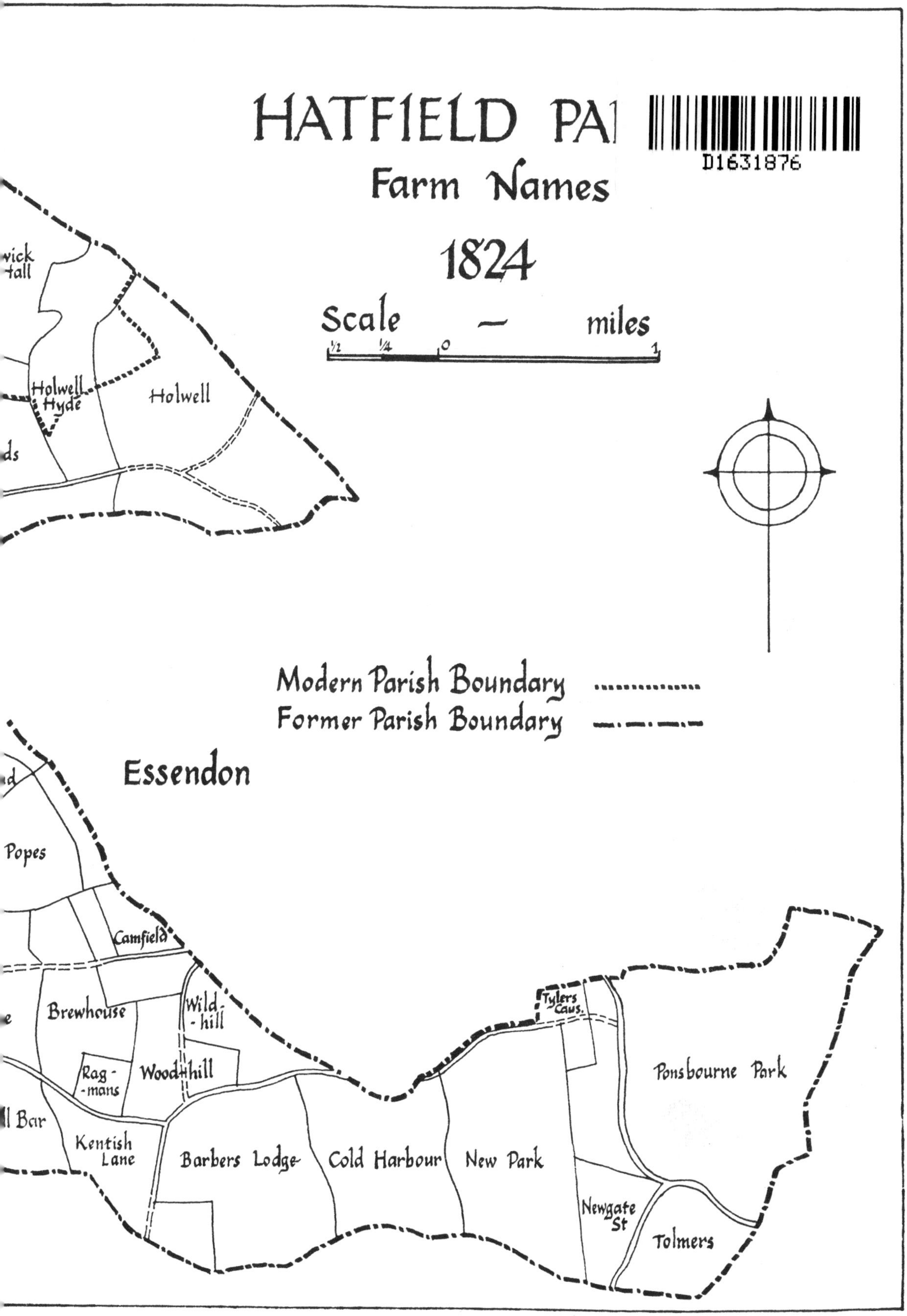

HATFIELD PA[RISH]

Farm Names

1824

Scale — miles

½ ¼ 0 1

Modern Parish Boundary ....
Former Parish Boundary —·—·—

Essendon

wick
Hall

Holwell
Hyde

Holwell

ds

Popes

Camfield

Brewhouse

Wild-
-hill

Rag-
-mans

Wood-hill

l Bar

Kentish
Lane

Barbers Lodge

Cold Harbour

New Park

Tylers
Caus.

Ponsbourne Park

Newgate
St

Tolmers

HATFIELD

A Pictorial History

View of Fore Street from Hatfield House Gateway

HATFIELD

A Pictorial History

Sue Kirby and Richard Busby

Phillimore

1995

Published by
PHILLIMORE & CO. LTD.
Shopwyke Manor Barn, Chichester, West Sussex

ISBN 0 85033 996 0

Printed and bound in Great Britain by
BIDDLES LTD.
Guildford, Surrey

List of Illustrations

Frontispiece: View of Fore Street from Hatfield House Gateway

Acknowledgements

Many people have assisted with the preparation of this book. In particular, we would like to thank the Marquess of Salisbury and the Librarian and Archivist at Hatfield House, Robin Harcourt-Williams; Rosemary Last, Librarian, Hatfield Library; Angela Eserin, Welwyn Garden City Local Studies Library; the *Welwyn and Hatfield Times*; H. John Gray; Henry W. Gray; Peter Clark, Hatfield Town Council; Dorothy and Eileen Larkin; Mr. J.R. and Mrs. O. Brown; David Spence; Robert Richardson; Mrs. D. Cann, secretary of Hatfield Concert Band and Ron Kingdon. Thanks are also due to all those who have given photographs to the Museum and Library over the years, especially Dennis Williams and Neil Jenkins, without whose generosity this book would not be possible. Last, but not least, thanks to Carol Rigby for her patience and good-will in word processing the text and re-working parts of it several times over!

Picture Acknowledgements

Author's collection, 1, 9, 41; Mrs. Barter, 146; British Aerospace, 124, 127, 137-8, 143, 152, 156, 164, 173; British Gas, 166; Mr. J.R. and Mrs. O. Brown, front endpaper, 30; Robert Capp, 110; J.P.B. Clarke, 142; Reg Coleman, 44, 165; Courtauld Institute, 10; Roger Eaton, 25; Jack Flegg, 67, 70, 100-1, 114; John French, Park Studios, 163; H. John Gray, 22, 80, 120, 131; Henry W. Gray, back endpaper; Miss K. Halsey, 136; Hatfield Library, 3-5, 7, 15-20, 23-4, 27-8, 37, 45, 48-9, 60, 62-5, 68-9, 74, 77, 79, 81-2, 88, 92, 94, 97, 102, 104-6, 108-9, 113, 115-17, 122, 128, 130, 132-3, 135, 139, 140-1, 144-5, 149, 153; Hertfordshire Constabulary, 111; *Herts. Advertiser*, 148; Hertfordshire County Council, 154-5; Herfordshire Record Office, 26, 61; Mrs. G. Hipgrave, 147; Ron Kingdon, 35, 71, 76, 83; Sue Kirby, 34, 85; Shirley Knapp, 40; Dorothy and Aileen Larkin, 98, 150; Marquess of Salisbury, 11, 12, 14; F. Mayo, 55; Dugald Mackay, 33; Mrs. C. Morriss, 118; Photomatic, 56; Robert Richardson, back end-paper; Malcolm Sawyer, 90-1; David Spence, 2; Studio Lisa, 129; The Tank Museum, Bovington, 121; *Times* Newspapers Ltd., 151; Mr. Warren, 87; Welwyn Garden City Library, 36, 51; Welwyn Hatfield District Council, 54; Welwyn Hatfield Museum Service, 6, 8, 21, 32, 38-9, 42, 46-7, 50, 52-3, 57-9, 66, 72-3, 75, 78, 84, 93, 95-6, 103, 107, 112, 119, 123, 125-6; *Welwyn & Hatfield Times*, 13, 29, 43, 86, 89, 99, 134, 157, 159, 167, 170-2, 174-6; Nigel Willoughby Photographic, 177; Ken Wright, Commission for the New Towns, 31, 158, 160-2, 168-9.

Introduction

To the casual visitor looking for evidence of Hatfield's past, it may appear that there is but little remaining. The fine parish church, Hatfield House, some picturesque houses and streets in the old town and Mill Green Watermill are well known. The name Hatfield has also been synonymous with the de Havilland Aircraft Co. and its successors for almost sixty years—now that too has gone. History itself is a record of change in a community and of the people and events that helped to shape it for better or worse.

This volume aims to record some of these changes and to give a flavour of the past, mainly in Hatfield itself, but also in some of the villages and hamlets forming the old ecclesiastical parish of Bishop's Hatfield (*see* endpapers). This includes Hatfield Hyde, Lemsford, Stanborough, Mill Green, Woodside, Wild Hill, Newgate Street, and Peartree and Handside, the latter two now districts of Welwyn Garden City. Each has its own story to tell.

Despite its proximity to the important Roman city of *Verulamium* (St Albans) and the smaller settlement at Welwyn, Hatfield has yielded few recorded early archaeological remains. Significant pre-Roman (mainly Iron Age or Belgic) burials have been found at Panshanger in Welwyn Garden City and at Welwyn village. In 1992 the remains of two or three hoards of late Iron Age artefacts, including weapons and gold coins, were found in a field near Essendon on what was possibly a sacred site. Scattered Roman remains have been found in parts of Welwyn Garden City, but Welwyn village has yielded sites of several villas one with two bathing suites, one of which is now preserved in a vault under the A1(M). Known Roman roads and pre-Roman trackways tended to pass near to, but rarely through, Hatfield, then still a densely wooded area traversed by the river Lea.

Domesday to Dissolution

By the time Domesday Book was being completed in 1086, there was a small settlement here, including at least two watermills, known as *Hetfelle*. The manor was then in the ownership of the Abbots (and later Bishops) of Ely—hence the origin of the older name 'Bishop's Hatfield' for the town. Here too the Bishops chose to build a palace, the first a timber-framed building, the second a fine, red-brick one completed in *c*.1480. It is the great hall of this building, erected by Bishop John Morton, that remains today as the Old Palace in the grounds of Hatfield House. Its location adjoining the old parish church of St Etheldreda was not, of course, mere chance.

By the middle of the 13th century clearance of woodland and its conversion to farmland had led to the creation of a number of smaller sub-manors or 'hides' within the parish, many of them moated sites. These included Cromer Hyde, Symondshyde, Durantshyde (now Brocket Park) and Astwick in the west and north; Handside, Ludwick, Holwell and Woodhall to the north and east and Popes, Ponsbourne and Tolmers to the south. Most of these were farms rather than large houses which later occupied several of these sites.

The medieval and Tudor town of Hatfield grew up on the hillside running down from the Bishop's Palace and the parish church. The present lines of Fore Street (or Front Street) and Church Street (formerly Back Street), Park Street (formerly Duck Lane), plus French Horn Lane and the former London and Great North Roads were established quite early. Several ale houses and inns grew up along these roads, amongst the earliest recorded being the *Chequers*, the *Cock* and the *George*—all long since demolished. Many more came later.

A fine old Market House once stood at the bottom of Fore Street, but was later removed to a site at the top of the street (*see* plate 61). The right to hold a market and fair was first granted by Henry III in 1226. Sadly little research has been done, and few physical remains have come to light, to give us an accurate picture of the town at this time. Excavations by the Hatfield and District Archaeological Society (HADAS) in the 1960s produced medieval pottery, some metalwork, glass and the leather sole of a child's shoe. These are now in the local museum at Mill Green, together with finds from the 17th to 19th centuries. Apart from the major buildings like the church and Old Palace, the most important evidence of a building of this period, of which remains survive, is the wattle and daub walling and old timbers in parts of Howe Dell School, formerly the Rectory.

In 1538 the long association with the Bishops of Ely ended abruptly when Henry VIII took ownership of their lands at Hatfield as part of an exchange for other former monastic properties. So it was that for the next seventy-five years or so the town became known as King's Hatfield. It was during this same period that the young Princess Elizabeth, under what we might now call 'house arrest', was kept at Hatfield until the death of her half-sister Mary in November 1558. The decayed remains of the oak tree, under which the princess is said to have been told of her accession to the throne, have recently been removed from the Park and indoors for their better preservation.

For several centuries the town remained one of small businesses and shops, a growing number of inns and ale houses, but little physical growth in population. By the middle of the 17th century there were some 1,200 people. There is documentary and archaeological evidence of a tannery near the eastern end of the old line of Batterdale, water coming from a stream or brook feeding at least two sizeable ponds. The smell of soaking animal skins and crushed bark can have been none too pleasant so near the town! Various maltings and breweries would also have produced their own distinctive smell. Between the 17th and end of the 19th centuries other local trades which flourished included silk and corn milling; brick making at Morrill Hill; paper and mill board making; straw plaiting and hat making and brewing. Beyond the immediate confines of the town area the local economy remained largely agriculturally based.

Great Estates

Like many other areas of the county, Hatfield was to rely heavily for its economic and social base on the owners of large estates and houses until at least the First World War.

It takes little imagination to appreciate that, from about 1611-12, the history of the area was inextricably linked to the presence of Hatfield House, home of the Cecil family to this day. Their management of the house and estate was largely a careful one, but as with all great families there were periods of decline, notably in the 18th century.

The history of Hatfield House and of the Cecil family has been well documented elsewhere. Suffice to say that Hatfield was the largest, but far from their only estate or property, either in Hertfordshire or beyond. Acquisition was piecemeal over several hundred years, so that by the end of the last century there was little going on in and around Hatfield that was not in some way connected with Lord Salisbury, or in which he and Lady Salisbury did not play some part. After all, many families and businesses owed their livelihood or patronage to his Lordship and his estate, lived in a property built and/or owned by him, or were directly or indirectly employed by the Estate. There is ample evidence of the family's humanity and generosity in its dealings with the local community.

For many years the grounds of Hatfield Park have been made accessible to local families as well as being host to the Hertfordshire Agricultural Show from 1911 to 1937 ; to the Tudor Revels and Elizabethan Pageants in the 1920s and '30s; to early tank trials during the First World War; to Home Guard training and reviews during the Second World War; to county rallies of scouts and guides and as home ground to Hatfield Cricket Club until 1923, then again from 1946 to 1979. In more recent times the estate has hosted mainly prestigious national events like the annual Living Crafts Fair and Festival of Gardening. All the above events were, of course, in addition to often large private garden parties, visits by foreign diplomats or royalty (notable during the times when the 3rd Marquess was Prime Minister) and visits by members of the British royal family, formal and informal, which continue to this day.

Within the parish there also stood a number of other fine houses, of which only one survives. The large house and estate known as Hatfield Woodhall (situated between Mill Green and the modern Stanborough Lake) was bought by Lord Salisbury (together with Stanboroughbury Farm) from the Rev. Julius Hutchinson for the huge sum then of £26,991 8s. 2d. (in October 1792). It was said once to have rivalled Hatfield House in splendour. It was demolished in or soon after 1792 and very little now remains. The surviving house is Brocket Hall, near Lemsford, completed c.1775 for the Lamb family. Its fine lake and Palladian bridge greatly enhance its riverside setting. Perhaps its most famous resident was Lady Caroline Lamb whose unrequited infatuation for the poet Byron led to the extremes of behaviour and illness that caused her husband and family such distress. Since then the house has been the home of two Prime Ministers—Melbourne (1779-1848) and Palmerston (1784-1865), a Viceroy of India, an Admiral of the Fleet and a Scottish-born millionaire. Since 1923 it has been owned by the Nall-Cain family and has recently been converted by Charles, Lord Brocket into an international conference centre, with golf course and many other facilities.

Road and Rail

Hatfield, like many other towns during the last 150 years, owes some of its past prosperity to its situation on the Great North Road. This was especially so during the 18th and early 19th centuries when many inns, ale houses and hostelries provided accommodation and refreshment to the increasing number of travellers by coach and horses. Then, the main road entered Hatfield at the top of Fore Street, after crossing

Hatfield Park, and left it past the *Wrestlers* pub and the turnpike gate near what was later Olding's Corner (now Tesco's). From there it passed through Stanborough and Lemsford and north via Brickwall Hill and the Ayot Green turnpike gate. Regular users, like those taking livestock to market, tried to avoid the tolls by using side roads and trackways and are recalled in the road name Drovers Way in Hatfield. Since about 1850 the line of the Great North Road has changed several times, and yet again in the 1980s when the A1(M) cut-and-cover tunnel was built.

Shortly before 1850 a great change was to take place, when the new main railway line from London to York was driven through Hatfield. Most welcomed its arrival as it not only revolutionised transport and travel to and from the town, but was to provide much needed local employment. It also gave rise to a further growth in public houses and, more importantly, to the development of the area now forming the commercial centre of the present town. It was to be known, appropriately, as Newtown and was to take on a character of its own. Coincidentally, it created something of a social division between the old and new town areas, with the railway dividing the two physically and socially (much as it was to do in Welwyn Garden City from the early 1920s onwards).

The siting of Hatfield station near the gates of Hatfield Park was one of the conditions imposed by Lord Salisbury, who had new gates constructed, a viaduct built over the Park Street area and was later to have his own private waiting room. By 1860 branch lines to Luton and Dunstable and another to Hertford had been added at the northern edge of the parish, and in 1865 a branch line to St Albans was opened. Hatfield thus became an important junction for Victorian and later travellers, although none of these branch lines survive except as attractive walks.

Parish and People

In 1851 the civil parish of Hatfield had a population of 3,862. Fifty years later it had increased by just under 900 people to 4,754 (less than 20 per cent), but within another fifty years it had risen by 38 per cent to some 12,500 in 1951. By 1991 this figure had more than doubled as the New Town's population reached 25,468. Since then the figures have shown little growth and recent projections suggest a small decline by 2001.

With this relatively slow, but steady, growth before 1950 when the new town was started, there came a need for not just more houses, but shops, churches, schools, water, gas and electricity supplies and local employment. In such a large ecclesiastical parish, five new Anglican churches were built within twenty-five years at Newgate Street (St Mary the Virgin, 1847); Woodhill (St Mark's, 1852, rebuilt 1880); Lemsford (St John's, 1858); St Luke's, Newtown (1877) and Hatfield Hyde (St Mary Magdalene's, 1882—which replaced the so called 'Mud Chapel' of 1861). Following the creation of the New Town in 1948, two other Anglican churches were built at Hilltop, South Hatfield (St John's, opened 1960) and Birchwood (St Michael's, opened 1955).

The earliest Nonconformist church to open was the classical-styled Park Street Baptist Chapel in the old town. Completed in 1823, it finally closed for services in 1932, when Christ Church, St Albans Road was opened. The Wesleyan Methodists met in a variety of places of worship before about 1851, when they occupied the inadequate, but appropriately named 'Moo Cow Chapel' near the top of Church Street. Nearly forty years later, and after much fund raising, a purpose-built church was opened in 1889 in French Horn Lane, but this was closed in 1938 when a new church was opened in Birchwood Avenue on 28 April. A second Methodist church later followed in Oxlease in 1962. At Lemsford, a small (unlicensed) brick-built Wesleyan chapel was opened in the 1870s, but was in use for barely fifty years before ending its days as a store-room; it was finally demolished in the 1960s.

The Roman Catholics had no purpose-built place of worship in Hatfield until February 1930, although there had been a Carmelite Convent of the *Deo Gratias* in a rather uninspiring concrete building near the site of the present church. Its enclosure was 'imposed' by Cardinal Bourne in July 1925 before he blessed the Convent, and he was to return a year later for another ceremony, the day before the new Roman Catholic church of St Bonaventure was opened in adjoining Welwyn Garden City. When the Convent left Hatfield, its buildings were demolished and a new Roman Catholic church and presbytery were opened in 1930. Some forty years later the present distinctive circular building named Marychurch replaced it. By then a second Roman Catholic church, St Peter's, had already been opened in Bishops Rise in 1961.

And so to school ...

Before the 1870 Education Act, Hatfield had the National (later London Road) School (built 1850), the Countess Anne Charity School (founded 1732), plus a number of small private schools. The latter occupied such diverse locations as Bush Hall (Jane Docwra); Northcotts (closed *c.*1860); The Rectory (now Howe Dell School); Triangle House, plus a few in Fore Street (one of which, founded *c.*1835, later moved to Puttocks Oak when Newtown was being developed). Outside Hatfield there were a number of small, mostly Church of England administered, schools at Ponsbourne (Newgate Street); Westfield (Woodhill); Hatfield Hyde and Lemsford. By 1905, the London Road School was too small and in that year St Audrey's School, for senior boys only, opened in Endymion Road. Girls were not admitted until 1924, remaining at London Road until then, together with the infants. In 1910-11 the average attendance was 192 girls and 130 infants, whilst the boy's average was 203.

Until the outbreak of war in 1914 a few other private schools came and went and those that survived had largely disappeared by the mid-1930s. Of these, perhaps the best known and oldest began life as a 'young gentleman's boarding school' in *c.*1870, founded by John Dare in Dagmar House, North Road. This was later to expand under Dare's adopted son, John R. Sheehan-Dare, into Hatfield Collegiate Schools; this was made up of Dagmar House (for boys) and adjoining Alexandra House (for girls). Under its last Principals, Mr. and Mrs. J.G. Prentice, it finally closed its doors in the early 1930s, and the buildings were demolished in the 1960s, when offices for Addo were built on the site. Another well-remembered small school was that in Galleycroft, run by the Misses Caesar in their home near the site of the present swimming pool. The first purpose-built County Council Schools were New Town Infant and Junior (opened 1933) and Green Lanes JMI (opened 1940). A nursery school was also opened in Birchwood at this time.

Following the Second World War and the designation of Hatfield as a New Town, rapid growth in housing and population meant that by the early 1960s some twenty County Council schools were open. Only in the 1980s and '90s, as school populations declined, were several of these closed or amalgamated, the buildings demolished, houses built on the sites or an alternative use found for them. Countess Anne is now the only old school surviving under its original name, as Onslow and St Audrey's have now amalgamated under one joint name.

In the area of further and adult education, classes, run at first by volunteers, were already well established by the 1890s. In 1940 the first Workers Educational Association classes were started; out of such classes in the 1950s grew the WEA Branch that was to publish the historical booklets *Hatfield and Its People*, and very recently the Hatfield This Century Group was formed to carry on where their predecessors, and the Hatfield and District Archaeological Society, had begun so successfully. The public library, and the more recently established Welwyn Hatfield Museum Service, have also done much to support or further the work of all the above.

In 1952 Hatfield Technical College was opened, beginning a steady growth in size and status, most recently becoming the University of Hertfordshire in 1992. Long before this, however, the institution had achieved a national reputation for the quality of its teaching, courses, seminars, research and for its Technical Information Service to Industry (HERTIS). Its more recent annual Technology Fair has also become a prestigious national event. In October 1970 the Association for Science Education opened its headquarters there.

And so to work ...

Industry has not figured largely in Hatfield's past with one notable exception. In 1933 Captain Geoffrey de Havilland and his co-directors decided to sell off their aircraft works at Stag Lane Aerodrome, Edgware. The aerodrome was boxed in by housing development and did not allow development of the larger aircraft then on the drawing board. They chose to construct a new factory at Hatfield where there was already a small grass airfield used by the London Aeroplane Club, adjoining the recently opened Barnet Bypass, and an area of flat farmland belonging to Harpsfield Hall Farm. The decision to acquire the land was to be a momentous one for the town, for the de Havilland Aircraft Company was to bring employment, training, prosperity and prestige to the area, as its own size and reputation grew.

It was run at first very much as a family business—'At one time, I had three sons, a brother, two nephews and a stepson in the firm', wrote Sir Geoffrey in his autobiography *Sky Fever*. He was quick to add, however, that he did not approve of such arrangements and that he expressly showed no favouritism to family members. They achieved on merit only. At its peak over 3,500 were employed there (that figure doubled during the Second World War) producing planes some of whose names were to become household words. Chief amongst them were the Comet, the wartime Mosquito bomber, Trident and, most recently, the HS and BAe 146.

Only in more recent decades, when the original company was taken over and production diversified into other areas such as rocketry, missiles and avionics, did Hatfield's rôle change and the slow and painful decline in the site's fortunes begin. Sixty years after its arrival the Hatfield factory closed its gates for ever on 24 December 1993 and its production arm transferred to Woodford, near Manchester. Meanwhile, the long-term future of the site and airfield remains uncertain.

If civil aircraft production dominated the local scene for six decades, smaller companies also made a vital contribution. Prior to 1920 there were a few family-owned businesses of a light industrial nature such as James Gray and W. Waters & Sons (carriage builders and motor engineers); Sherriff & Sons (Lemsford (water) Mill); Alfred John Starkey, Mill Green (smith and agricultural engineer); George Lovell (blacksmith and beer retailer, Newtown) and the Pryor Reid Brewery, near the centre of the old town. Of a more traditionally based nature were businesses like Hollier's

Dairy; Edmund Payne, printer in Park Street; the watercress growers Benjamin Eagles and George Timms, at Lemsford and the water mills at Mill Green (closed *c.*1911) and Essendon.

Between the two World Wars the greatest impact on employment, apart from the arrival of de Havilland's, was undoubtedly the arrival of nearby Welwyn Garden City. In Hatfield itself, however, two companies with important new factories opened almost simultaneously in the 1930s. These were S.L.D. (Jack) Olding (Agricultural machinery and caterpillar track makers) at Mount Pleasant in 1939 and M. Cook & Son (cardboard carton and packaging maker) off Green Lanes in 1937 (later Cook's Corrugated Cases, U.K. Corrugated and now Smurfit Corrugated). The former closed in 1985 and the building, with its famous façade, was demolished to make way for Tesco and other superstores.

Shortly after the Second World War ended and reconstruction began, factories like Olding's and DH's, which had changed over to wartime production, returned to their former rôle, whilst other smaller businesses set up temporarily on sites such as the former Mill Green Camp; at Welham Green and in Welwyn Garden City. When the latter and Hatfield were designated as New Towns in 1948, industrial sites were earmarked on the Master Plans. Over the next twenty-five years many companies were attracted to Hatfield, amongst them Lone Star Products; Polaroid U.K.; Budget Rent-a-Car; Davall Gear Co; Liebherr Ltd; Furniglass; Stafford-Miller Pharmaceuticals and Welham Plant Hire (now Mabey's). More recent arrivals have included Mitsubishi; Turbine Services; Hatfield Construction; Nippodenso (UK) Ltd. and Halla (UK) Ltd. New sites have also been established near Hatfield station as well as in Hatfield Business Park on the former Hawker Siddeley Dynamics site.

Shops and Shopping

For at least six centuries local commerce thrived on small family-owned shops and a regular weekly market. These in turn were also supported by the owners of the large estates and houses where appropriate. Communities were very self sufficient and, even into the early years of this century, poorer people rarely, if ever, travelled beyond the parish. Shops with once familiar names like Tingey's (grocers); Walby's (butchers); Dollimore (greengrocer); Daisy Gray (stationers); Hall and Hulks (bakers); Hankin's and A.E. Sharp (both drapers); Cox (chemist) and Olive Lusty's (sweets, tobacco) have all gone. Others began small, but later developed far beyond their original Hatfield premises; for example, Sid Rumbelow's (radio and television); Hill & Simmons, now Simmons Bakery (Hatfield) Ltd.

Only since the 1980s has the steady decline of small shops taken place in Hatfield as elsewhere. The development of 'out of town' superstores began here in 1985 when Tesco's were given permission to build such a store on the Olding's site at Mount Pleasant. The new superstore opened on 9 February 1988 when their town centre store closed. Soon afterwards Homebase and Habitat, and later Comet, joined Tesco on the Olding's site. This development not only changed people's shopping habits, but also led to more widespread Sunday opening.

However, Hatfield's first 'superstore' was built in the town centre some sixteen years earlier, when Woolco opened in 1972. Whilst the building itself did little to enhance the town centre, the store enjoyed reasonable success for some fifteen years. In 1987 the store was refurbished by Gateway, but they only stayed until 1990 when ASDA acquired the site.

For those areas away from the town centre, the Hatfield Development Corporation (later Commission for the New Towns) planned neighbourhood shopping areas at Hilltop, Cavendish and Birchwood in the 1950s and 1960s. These complemented existing ones at Manor Parade, St Albans Road East and Harpsfield Broadway. Some of these have enjoyed mixed fortunes in recent years after their early success, unable to compete or forced out by rent increases. Village and mobile shops have enjoyed similar ups and downs, few surviving to the present day. Hatfield Market Traders have also tried to extend their activities with a Sunday Market since 1993 to meet competition and changing shopping habits. Even the town's main post office has not remained unaffected, having moved in 1993 to shop premises, part of Martin the Newsagent.

The other dramatic change to shopping in Hatfield began some ten years ago in 1984 when the Carroll Group of companies obtained permission to erect a huge, covered shopping plaza over the proposed A1(M) Tunnel. This controversial £200 million development, known initially as Park Plaza, was the subject of a Public Enquiry in 1985 and engendered much opposition from local traders and other developers, as well as neighbouring District Councils. After much publicity and delays in building, the complex finally opened on 12 September 1991 as The Galleria. Based on an American concept, The Galleria contained 130 small shop units, mixed with six restaurants or fast-food outlets, a children's skating rink-cum-entertainment area and generous car parking facilities. Promoted as the 'ultimate shopping experience', it was conceived as a place where you could shop in ease and comfort in pleasant, dry and warm surroundings, and enjoy light refreshments or a meal during or after shopping hours. The development also included a nine-screen UCI Cinema, with adjacent eat-in/drive-in McDonald's and a Deep Pan Pizza restaurant. At weekends especially, free entertainment was staged in the central plaza, be it live music or dance, an exhibition or crazy golf.

The Galleria was a bold concept, which in less uncertain financial times might have been more secure. Despite every effort to promote it widely, income failed to match expectation; units opened and closed with noticeable regularity; there was no large 'anchor store' to attract customers, and this despite generous opening times at weekends and in the evenings. A year after opening, the operators placed The Galleria into receivership in September 1992 and sought a new buyer, whilst continuing to trade. In October 1993 Waxy Management, on behalf of Dutch clients, acquired the complex for a reported £10.5 million and the future of The Galleria was again secured.

And so to play...
The pursuit of leisure interests, or simply 'having fun', is obviously nothing new. From the simple street and ball games to the masques and banquets held at the great houses, rich and poor alike found their own level of amusement. From the time Bishop Morton built his palace at Hatfield over 500 years ago, both that and the present house and Park were the scene of banquets, plays, masques, dances and other sports and entertainment.

The first Marchioness of Salisbury, Irish-born Emily Mary (1750-1835), was a good example of the fun-loving aristocratic lady, with a taste for sports and for entertaining in lavish style. In addition to a liking for card games, the Marchioness became an enthusiastic exponent of archery by the 1790s. Together with Stephen Sullivan of nearby Ponsbourne Manor, she was a founder member and patron of the Hertfordshire Society of Archers. Sadly, her own dramatic death in a fire at Hatfield House in 1835 was to bring her a very different type of audience. Household accounts for the Cecil estates (Hatfield; Quickswood, near Clothall, Herts. and Salisbury House in London) for the 1630s show that William Cecil, the second Earl, was spending some £2,500 a year on his pantry alone. This equates to about a quarter of a million pounds in modern money. Not all the Earls of Salisbury, however, were able to spend on this scale.

Horse-racing and ownership has traditionally been a rich man's pursuit. Locally, the best known early 19th-century follower of the sport was Peniston Lamb, Viscount Melbourne of Brocket Hall. It was Lamb who laid out his own race-course around the north and east side of his house (now part of the new golf course). Here Lamb and his wealthy London friends, including George, the Prince Regent (later George IV), amused themselves and their ladies between parties, dances, hunting and gambling.

Another local man from Hatfield Hyde, Joseph Farrah, farmer and coal merchant, also tried to capitalise on horse racing. After challenging the 'sporting gentlemen of all England' to race one of his cobs over two or four miles for £25 to £100 in June 1833, his venture failed. By November his farming stock and 'a capital racing cob *Lucksall*' were for sale and Farrah was declared bankrupt!

Reference has already been made to the long association of cricket with Hatfield Park. Real tennis was also played there from the mid-19th century. In the late 1920s and '30s Lord Salisbury employed one Alfred Lambert as a 'Tennis Professional'. A Joseph Lambert (died 1903) had played on the first real tennis courts at Hatfield House and other members of his family were also involved. His son (Charles) George Lambert (1842-1914) became a world champion real tennis player between 1871 and 1885, whilst another son William, played for Middlesex County Cricket Club as well as being a real tennis professional. Public lawn tennis courts included the 'Showfield' site near the present District Council offices in St Albans Road East. Hatfield Lawn Tennis & Bowls Club was founded in 1924.

Football has been played on an organised basis in Hatfield since at least the 1880s, when both senior and junior teams existed in the area. The Mid Herts Football League was founded in 1892. Until 1906, Dagmar House Old Boys FC (founded 1900) and Hatfield FC played separately, but in 1901 amalgamated to become Hatfield United FC. By September 1908 the former striped jerseys of the town club had been replaced with plain Cambridge blue jerseys and dark blue shorts. The Club's ground was the former Herts Agricultural Showground site off Ground Lane, where from 1920 it had its own changing rooms and stand. The Cadets played on 'Canham's Field', adjoining the *Gun* public house in Newtown. To confuse matters further, in 1922 some of the Football and Cricket Club members joined forces to form the Hatfield United Athletic Club, concentrating mainly on cross country running, gymnastics and drill, but later with lawn tennis and hockey sections as well. Like all football clubs, Hatfield's saw its good and bad seasons, but it was to win local challenge cups on many occasions and a number of its players and officials went on to become capped county players or referees. One member, William A Groom (1890-1959), became a real tennis professional.

Hatfield's first public swimming pool was at Mill Green, where part of the river was widened to make a simple bathing area in the 1920s. Not until 1966, when the present swimming pool was opened at the junction of Lemsford Road and Cavendish Way, did the town have a pool built to modern standards. A wholesale renovation and refurbishment completed in 1991 provided an improved fitness suite and the other facilities of a modern swim centre.

The first films to be shown in Hatfield were occasional screenings at the Public Hall in London Road between 1913 and 1925; the Union Workhouse was also licensed from 1913 to show films. In mid-1925 the Public Hall became the Picture House, and by 1928 was showing films up to three days a week. The first purpose-built cinema was the Regent in Common Lane (now The Common), opened in 1935. Following varying changes of ownership and fortunes, it became known successively as the Odeon, the Classic, the Curzon and the Chequers between 1943 and 1969, when it finally closed. It has since been the Chequers Bingo and Social Club. Only since the opening of the UCI near The Galleria on 27 September 1991 has Hatfield had its own cinema again—a far remove from its modest predecessors. Ironically, however, there were plans in 1935 to build an 1,800-seat cinema, with ballroom, cafe, shops and parking for 1,000 cars very near the UCI site.

For those preferring more strenuous indoor activities, the Hatfield Sports and Leisure Centre was opened in Travellers Lane in 1973, and is operated currently by the District Council. On the other side of town near the Birchwood Estate, the Hatfield Town Council opened a new Sports and Community Centre in Longmead in 1992, although not without some local opposition.

Golfers were not well served locally until after the Second World War. Hatfield residents had to go to Welwyn Garden City or Brookmans Park and only in very recent years have two private courses opened within the old parish area—at Brocket Hall and at Mill Green.

The town's youth have been well served for many years by the two largest clubs— The Break's (best known for the annual pantomime) and Downs Farm, although the latter lost its clubhouse when its site near Hilltop was redeveloped in 1989. It now shares recreational facilities incorporated into the Jim MacDonald Community Centre in Highview, opened by the District Council in April 1990. Most of the local churches began youth clubs in the late 1950s and '60s in response to the demands of the New Town population growth. Drug abuse was also becoming a growing problem at this time in the area.

For adults of all ages social and community clubs and facilities have been provided for well over a century, catering for all levels and kinds of interest. Prior to 1914 these were as varied as Clothing Clubs, the Church of England Temperance Society, the Dickens Fellowship; a Rifle Club; the Hatfield Working Men's Club and a Masonic Lodge. Since the coming of the New Town in 1948, the Development Corporation, and its successor the Commission for the New Towns, made great efforts to foster and promote community activities, in conjunction with existing bodies, both official and amateur, paid and voluntary. During the next thirty-five years the New Town saw the building of Cavendish Hall; Hilltop complex; Friendship House; Oxlease Hall; the Hyde Hall, Hatfield Hyde and Lemsford Village Hall amongst others. Several new churches also had halls and meeting rooms attached to them. Finally, two major local authority projects have catered for very different interests. In September 1970 Welwyn Garden City UDC opened the 126-acre artificial lake and public park at Stanborough, which, as well as being a picnic, walking and recreation area, has sailing and watersurfing facilities and tuition; a swimming pool; an annual water carnival, firework displays and other events. A plan to extend the facilities towards Mill Green in the 1980s (known as the Haven Green Project) did not come to fruition. The second important facility, built and operated by the Welwyn Hatfield District Council, was the opening of the

Forum Theatre and Leisure Centre in Lemsford Road, Hatfield in 1975. This has provided a wide variety of events, from performances by local or county youth orchestras and choirs to professional performers and groups both individually or in pantomime, music hall, jazz and dance bands, magic shows, etc. The Hatfield Philharmonic Chorus and the Hatfield Concert Band are amongst local musical performers here and on the national circuit.

Hatfield is a town with both historic and contemporary interest and at the centre of what was one of the largest ecclesiastical parishes in England. Like many places, it is twinned with another European town, Zieriksee in the Netherlands (since 1953). The fact that much of the visible evidence of Hatfield's past is gone makes this book all the more important as a brief record for present and for future generations.

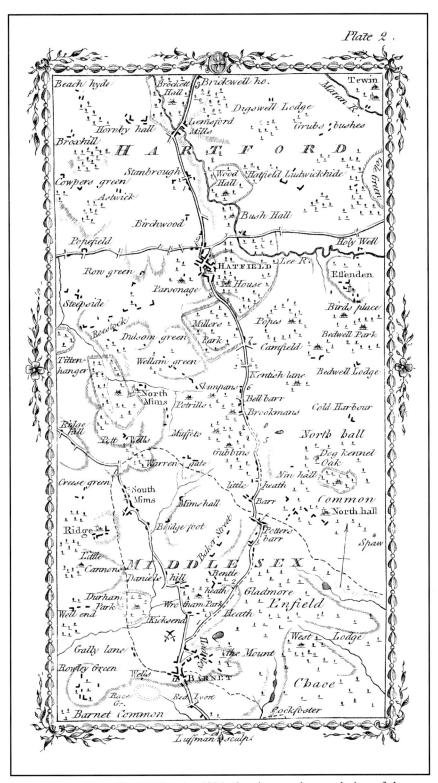

1 Map by John Luffman printed *c.*1806, showing an elongated view of the area covered by Hatfield parish, from Bell Bar ('at the XVIIth Milestone') in the south, to Brocket Park and Brickwall House in the north. The Great North Road follows its old line, determined between *c.*1770 and 1850. This was much changed with the coming of the railway in 1850. In the north at Lemsford Mills, the village was not bypassed until some twenty-five years after this map was published.

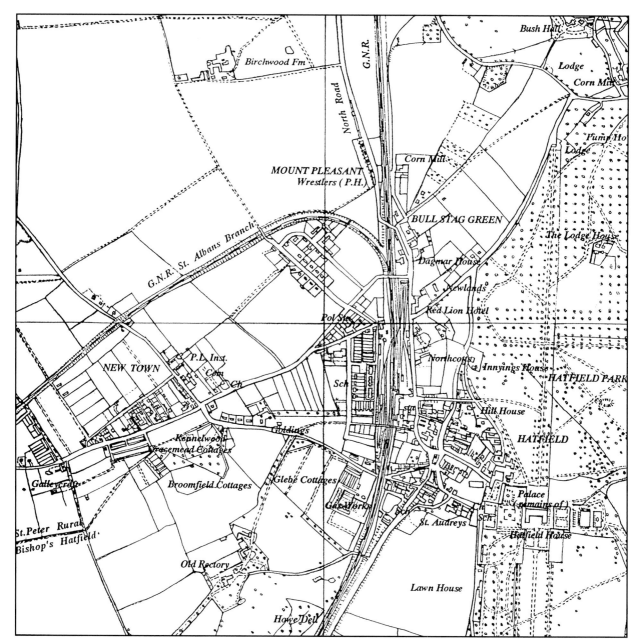

2 This map, based on the Ordnance Survey 6-inch map of Hertfordshire XXXV NE 1925, shows Hatfield House and the old town just to its north. West of the Great Northern Railway is New Town, the speculative development built in advance of the railway in 1848. Just over a century later it became the post-war New Town centre. The area at this time was still largely rural. Part of the hamlet of Mill Green can be seen in the top right-hand corner.

3 This 1803 view of St Etheldreda's shows the church before it was much altered later in the century, when parts were rebuilt and it was re-roofed and a spire added. At this time the nave walls were four feet lower, most of the windows contained plain glass, the flooring was old and uneven and inside there was a gallery for schoolchildren and the organ was at the west end.

4 In 1847 the spire on the church was new and many of the older buildings in Back Street (now Church Street), North Road and Batterdale remained. The *Salisbury Arms Tap* is clearly visible at the top of Fore Street. The square timber-framed building, centre foreground, is the *Dray Horse* public house. The site of the *Salisbury Temperance Hotel* adjoining it to the right was then still old cottages with, to its right, the site of the old workhouse yard on which cottages for the Hartfordshire Militia were shortly to be built.

5 These splendid reclining figures in the Brocket Chapel of Hatfield parish church are (*rear*) Elizabeth (d.1612), second wife of Sir John Brocket (d.1598) of Brocket Hall, who was twice Sheriff of Hertfordshire; and (*front*) Dame Agnes Sanders (d.1588), mother of Elizabeth by the second of her three husbands, Roger Moore of Burcester, Oxfordshire. Dame Agnes' genealogy is recorded in a curious rhyming inscription (not shown) below the figures. Because Sir John died without a male heir, his estates in Hatfield passed through his daughters to the Reade family and out of Brocket ownership for over 300 years.

6 The Church Lads' Brigade was founded in 1891. This photograph of *c*.1912 shows the Hatfield Brigade. It was taken in the garden of the St Audrey's Rectory in Church Street. In the centre is the bearded and much-loved Rector, Lord William Gascoyne-Cecil, son of the 3rd Marquess, who left Hatfield to become Bishop of Exeter in 1916. On his right is the Rev. C.T.T. Wood, one of the parish's curates from 1908, who won the Military Cross in the First World War and became Archdeacon of St Albans in 1942.

7 St Etheldreda's Church choir, *c.*1916. This photograph is of special interest for including the departing Rector Lord William Cecil (bearded, centre) shortly to become Bishop of Exeter; his successor the Rev. J. Antrobus (on his right) and the Rev. C. T. T. Wood, senior curate, who later won the Military Cross. Also shown, members of the Whitby, Walby, Kentish, Richardson, Titmuss, Dunham, Gray, Gartside, Rowlatt, Taylor, Vodden, Panter, Birch, Wilson and Bayliss families and choirmaster and organist, Harold W. Harrison.

8 This aerial photograph of *c.*1925 shows the south front of Hatfield House (and its original entrance), the East and West Gardens, parkland, the Old Palace and St Etheldreda's Church with its spire of wooden shingles (removed in 1930). Nearby the Georgian buildings of Fore Street, Park Street and the Wesleyan Chapel and graveyard, Chapman's Yard, the red-brick viaduct over the street with the appropriately named Hill House in its shadow. The latter was probably built by William Hall (d.1845), a local builder and landowner, whose family was distantly related by marriage to Sir Geoffrey de Havilland.

9 The Hertfordshire Society of Archers was founded by Emily Mary, the first Marchioness of Salisbury (1750-1835), whose great love of outdoor pursuits and entertaining became legendary. The above print from the *Ladies Pocket Book* (1791) includes the Duchess of Leeds; the Hon. Miss Charlotte Grimston of Gorhambury, St Albans; Miss Henrietta Sebright of Beechwood House, near Hatfield and Lady Salisbury. Note the fashionable tall hats worn by the ladies and the French-style target with nine colour circles instead of the modern five.

10 James Brownlow William Gascoyne-Cecil, 2nd Marquess of Salisbury (1791-1868), wanted to become a professional soldier, but was prevented by his parents from doing so. He did, however, succeed his father as Colonel and Commanding Officer of the Hartfordshire Militia from May 1816 until his death on 13 April 1868. At Hatfield he built housing for the sergeants of the Militia in Salisbury Square (*see* plate 87). He also began evening classes for boys on the estate and did much to improve both Hatfield House and tenants' housing in his ownership. New farming methods were another of his interests. Twice married, he had 12 children. The above portrait by John Lucas, painted in 1844, shows the Marquess in the robes of a Knight of the Garter.

11 Lady Gwendolen Cecil (1860-1945) was the second of the two daughters of the third Marquess and was known in the family as T.T. With her sister and five brothers, she had a happy and fairly free upbringing at Hatfield, where she lived all her 85 years. Giving much of her time to her distinguished father's career and interests, she is best remembered locally for her many charitable activities, especially in support of the underprivileged and mentally ill. She was also given to designing practical inventions; the platform step with handrail, just visible beside the car in the photograph, may well have been of her devising. She lived most of her life in the Lodge House, Home Park, near the Hertford Road Gate of Hatfield Park. With their aunt are George Edward Cecil (1895-1914), Beatrice Cecil (1891-1980), who became Lady Harlech, and Mary Cecil (1895-1988), who became Duchess of Devonshire.

12 1946 and four generations of the Cecil family come together to celebrate the birth of a future heir to the Estate. *Standing left*: James, the 4th Marquess (1861-1947); *right*: Robert, who became the 5th Marquess (1892-1972). *Seated*: Robert, Lord Cranborne, now the 6th and present Marquess, with his son Robert Michael James Cecil (the present Lord Cranborne).

13 H.M. Queen Elizabeth the Queen Mother has made frequent official and private visits to Hatfield House over the last fifty years. Here Her Majesty is seen in 1988, with Lady Salisbury with whom she shares a common interest in gardens. Lady Salisbury has done much to enhance and restore the gardens at Hatfield House to their former splendour and variety; she has also written a book entitled *The Gardens of Queen Elizabeth the Queen Mother* and a guide *The Gardens at Hatfield House*.

14 The 6th and present Marquess of Salisbury standing beside the last remains of the famous Hatfield Oak, 17 November 1978. History has it that the young Princess Elizabeth was sitting under this tree reading, when on 17 November 1556 news reached her of her succession to the throne. Shortly afterwards the new queen held her first Council of Ministers in the Great Hall at Hatfield.

15 George F. Hulks, coachman to Mr. and Mrs. H.J.B. Kendall of The Hyde, Hatfield Hyde, waits outside the main gates of Hatfield House, *c.*1908. Behind him the statue by George Frampton, sculptor, of the 3rd Marquess of Salisbury and former Prime Minister, unveiled in October 1906. Mr. Hulks had previously been coachman to the Busks of Codicote Lodge, Herts. and also worked for Lord Salisbury. He served in the RASC during the Second World War and in later years lived at Church Cottage, Hatfield Hyde and did much for his local church.

16 This unique photograph of the domestic staff at Hatfield House, taken during the time of the 3rd Marquess (d.1903), was rescued from the dustbin of a local house a few years ago. Probably taken between *c*.1890-95, the names of the 24 staff are not known as no record of domestic or house staff was kept at this time. The photograph clearly includes the butler, housekeeper, cooks, footmen, valets, personal maids and parlour-maids.

17 (*above*) The efficient management and maintenance of a large estate like Hatfield House was very important and required good organisation and a sizeable staff. Apart from the gardens and home farm, there was woodland to be managed, fences and boundary walls to be maintained, buildings and grounds maintenance, carpentry work, stables and carriages to be cared for and much more. This photograph of the estate staff in *c*.1920 shows 38 men and boys including gardeners, carpenters, gamekeepers, foresters, cowmen and stable lads.

18 (*above*) On Friday 13 June 1800 Hatfield Park was host to a review of the Hartfordshire Regiment of Militia by King George III and members of the Royal Family. Preparations began at Easter and by 16 May all the county volunteer units had been reviewed by Lord Salisbury. The 2nd Marquess of Salisbury, as Commanding Officer and Lord Lieutenant of Hertfordshire, also oversaw the detailed arrangements. The king and his entourage arrived in coaches at Hatfield with their escort at 9.00 a.m., but the volunteers were in place some one-and-a-half hours earlier, including the Hatfield Troop of Infantry with 77 men in blue jackets and white waistcoats, under Captain Penrose. In all over 1,060 officers and men were being reviewed. After breakfast at the House, and as the king mounted his horse, the Yeomanry Cavalry fired a 21-gun royal salute. The Royal Party then rode down the North Avenue, past the Elizabeth Oak to the front line, the king on horseback, the remainder in open carriages. A march past and general salute of three volleys ended the formal proceedings. Dinner for the Royal Party and all the volunteers was taken at 21 tables set out in the Park. The King left at 4.30 p.m., much pleased with his visit. The detail above is from a print of the painting by Richard Livesay.

19 (*left*) Members of the Hatfield branch of the Dickens Fellowship joined representatives of branches from all over the country for this group photograph taken at Hatfield House during the Fellowship's Annual Conference, 26-27 June 1926. As a journalist with the *Morning Chronicle*, Charles Dickens (1812-1870) visited Hertfordshire in 1835 to report on a fire which destroyed part of Hatfield House. He used various references to Hertfordshire in several of his novels.

20 The Tudor Revels and Elizabethan Pageants became regular events in Hatfield Park between 1924 and 1937. The original idea seems to have come from local businessman and County Councillor, F.W. Speaight. Leading parts were often taken by members of the Cecil family, their relations and friends and other local landowning families. Everyone entered into the spirit of the event and dressed appropriately; local schoolchildren performed maypole dances. Money raised went to various local schools or charities.

21 H.R.H. the Duchess of York is welcomed by nearly 2,000 guides and 6,000 visitors during a County Rally at Hatfield House on Saturday, 13 June 1931. The rally was held to raise funds towards the New Imperial Headquarters of the Girl Guides Association. A historical pageant was also performed which included re-enactments of episodes in Hatfield's past. With the Duchess of York in the photograph is Mrs. Wolverley Fordham of Ashwell, County Commissioner for Hertfordshire, and immediately behind them is Lord Hampden.

22 Lord Salisbury's XI at Hatfield Park cricket ground, Sunday, 10 June 1956. (*left to right*): Lord Robin Balniel (local M.P. and 12th man); Patrick Petrie; Hon Patrick Lindsay; Denis Compton; Fred Titmus (who ran a newsagent's shop in Hatfield Garden Village); W. J. 'Bill' Edrich (who lived in Green Lanes, Hatfield at the time); Lord Salisbury; John Murray; R.V.C. Robins; Leslie Compton; Earl de la Warr (former Postmaster General); J.J. Warr and Lord Kilmuir (Lord Chancellor). They were playing A.C.L. Bennett's XI in a charity match to raise funds for Hatfield Youth Centre. Lord Salisbury's XI lost by only 11 runs.

23 Brocket Hall was designed *c.*1750-1 for Sir Matthew Lamb M.P., but was not completed until after his death in 1768. Of an earlier house, referred to from the 1560s as 'Watershypps', nothing remains; similarly of 'a Chappel adjoining the Keepers House ...' mentioned in a document of 1720. The present house, together with the fine bridge and waterfall at the southern end of the lake, was designed by James Paine (1716-89). Built of red brick, the house contains some fine decorated plaster ceilings, an elegant main staircase and other furnishings and fittings. Apart from its well-known associations with Lady Caroline Lamb, it was later the home of two Prime Ministers, the second Lord Melbourne (d.1848 and buried in a vault in Hatfield Church) and his brother-in-law Lord Palmerston (d.1865). Both died at Brocket Hall. It was acquired in 1923 by Charles Alexander Nall-Cain, created 1st Baron Brocket in 1933, in whose family it currently remains.

24 Bush Hall appears to have been a farmhouse, with adjoining water mill, for many years and in 1574-7 had 120 acres of parkland. During the last 150 years it has been leased by Lord Salisbury to a wide variety of tenants. Amongst them was Sir Robert Chester (d.1848), Master of Ceremonies to Kings George III, George IV, William IV and Queen Victoria; H.J.B. Kendall (d.1914); Arthur Lewis Stride (d.1922) and Lt. Col. R.N. Greenwood M.C. On 1 January 1941 the house became a Red Cross Hospital (Red Cross Detachment Herts. 6), with Miss Elizabeth Bennett as Commandant and a dedicated team of mainly young nurses. Wounded patients from Dunkirk and North Africa and badly burned pilots, some from Archibald McIndoe's pioneering plastic surgery unit, were amongst those nursed here. After the war it became a private school in the 1950s and is now a hotel and country club.

25 A mile and a half south of Hatfield House, Pope's Manor was first occupied in the 13th century. The Pope family, who gave the manor its name, acquired the house in 1396. Successive families altered and enlarged it. The gardens were landscaped in 1722. Shortly afterwards the house burned down and it was rebuilt in 1750. In 1815 the property, described as a freehold estate comprising 'the Manor of Popes with spacious elegant Mansion seated in a Park and 1,070 acres of land, annual value £1,400', was put up for sale but failed to find a buyer. It was subsequently sold privately to James, the 1st Marquess of Salisbury, in 1817. The building was then demolished. Roger Eaton's drawing combines both archaeological and literary evidence to reconstruct Popes Manor as it might have appeared in 1790 during the occupancy of Sir Benjamin Truman. In front of the house was a small formal garden adjoining the slightly larger natural or wilderness garden. The house sale notice describes the outbuildings as 'detached offices' consisting of 'a dairy, brewhouse, wash-house, gardeners room, standing for four carriages, stables for 12 horses' and notes that the 'Farmyard contains 2 barns, dove-house, piggery, poultry house, cow houses and dog kennels etc.'.

26 Woodside Place was rebuilt *c.*1770 by local 'rags to riches' man John Church (d.1788); a Tudor house had formerly stood on the site. The above view is from a drawing dated 1839 by J.C. Buckler. Later owners of the house included Sir William Selby Church (1837-1928), an eminent physician and lecturer and Chairman of Hatfield Rural District Council from 1901-19. His eldest son, John William Church (1874-1918), was tragically killed in the last months of the First World War. During the Second World War the house was an RAF Warrant Officers' and Sergeants' Mess for 239 Squadron. It is now a country club.

27 Tolmers, Newgate Street takes its name from the 13th-century family of de Tolymer, tenants of the Bishop of Ely. Until about 1550 its history is uncertain, but it was then held by William Parr, brother of Catherine Parr, Henry VIII's last wife. After this it had a large number of owners or tenants; in the last century its owners included two M.P.s, Thomas Mills (d.1847) and Thomas Bazley (d.1885), the latter having the house altered and enlarged to its present size and appearance. After becoming a private school from c.1920-37 it was used as a military hospital during the last war, then as a County Council home for the elderly.

28 Great Nast Hyde dates from the late 16th- early 17th-century and is built in an 'H' form. Inside are some fine fireplaces and panelling and the bell turret contains a half cwt. bell made by John Warner in 1913 (or 1918). Prior to 1538 the estate belonged to the Abbey of St Albans and remained as a farm for many years. After passing to the Kentish family, in the present century it has been occupied by Ernest Schenk; the Hart-Dyke family up until c.1920 and by L.E. Janson, who later built 'The Breaks' in Hatfield (see plate 153). During the Second World War it was requisitioned for military use and was afterwards used by the de Havilland Aircraft Company as a guest house.

29 In the 18th and 19th centuries Stanborough Farm prospered as a large and well managed sheep farm. In 1825, when this print was made, it was owned by Thomas Cox, whose surviving account books give interesting details of farm practices and wages. From the 1860s to 1880s William James Webb was farmer here, but saw a gradual change from sheep to arable and root vegetable production as lamb imports from New Zealand and Australia flooded the market.

30 Birches or Birchwood probably takes its name from the 13th-century family of de la Birch(e), the farm itself developing early out of four common fields. According to Arthur Young's *Survey of Hertfordshire Agriculture* (published in 1804), the Pratchett family at Birchwood (who were also licensees of the *Eight Bells* public house from the 1760s), grew mainly turnips for fodder. The farm's last owners were the Crawfords (father and son, both named Daniel), who first came here in 1892. They did much to modernise and improve the buildings and management of the land.

31 This was the earliest of the two Roe Green Farms, known as Roe Green North, Hollier's or Hill's Farm. In 1773 the farm was sold to Edward Willis, the Bishop of Bath and Wells. It was farmed by his son Captain John Willis, who may have been responsible for enlarging the farmhouse. Almost a century later, the 3rd Marquess of Salisbury purchased the property. It was eventually acquired by the Development Corporation. Georgian House, as the yellow-washed brick farmhouse became known, was demolished in 1966. Its last tenant was Mr. F.J. Hollier, who kept a fine herd of Guernsey cows supplying milk for the family's local dairy business.

32 Several Scottish farmers were brought to Hatfield by Lord Salisbury in the last century, including James Sinclair in 1863. Their farm of 400 acres known as Harpsfield Hall remained essentially arable under the Sinclairs and was complimented in 1901 when visited by author H. Rider Haggard whilst researching his book *Rural England*. The farmhouse itself was demolished after de Havillands took over the land for their airfield in 1934. The Sinclairs paid above national wage rates and at harvest time women and boys were employed in addition to the regular farm workers and casual labour. This photograph of *c*.1900 includes Sinclair's foreman John Grovestock.

33 Scottish farmers first came to Hertfordshire and the other home counties in the early 19th century. The Great Depression from 1875 to 1899 encouraged the migration of dairy farmers from Scotland at a time when farms were being converted from arable to grass because of the serious drop in the price of corn. The same factors applied during the depression following the First World War. Mr. Dugald Mackay, pictured here *c.*1943 with his prize Ayrshire cow— 'Orange Bud', came from Bruchag, Rothesay in 1923 and farmed at Garston, Watford before taking Symondshyde as tenant of Lord Salisbury in 1932. He and his brother Willie, of the adjoining Suttons Farm, won many prizes for their dairy herds.

34 Ascots Farm was only built by Lord Salisbury in 1912-13 on land known as Leggs Charity Land. Its first tenant was Wilfred F. Sheriff, son of Arthur J. Sheriff (d.1921), who kept pedigree Berkshire pigs and cattle there. In the late 1920s and early '30s it was farmed by J.H. Robinson, until being leased to F.J. Hollier & Sons dairy of Goldings Farm, French Horn Lane, Hatfield (q.v., *see* plate 35). The photograph was taken shortly before the demolition of the buildings in Ascots Lane, now on the edge of Welwyn Garden City. Some of the farm buildings were badly damaged during the Second World War and had to be rebuilt.

35 F.J. Hollier & Sons opened their dairy at Goldings Farm in French Horn Lane shortly after the First World War. Their milk carts and floats were to become a common sight in the area for over fifty years. Before the Hollier family acquired it, Goldings had served as Hatfield's police station from 1856 to 1883 (*see* plate 109), then reverted to being a farm under the Humphreys family until the First World War. Between 1909-32 Miss Ada Norman ran a private school at West Goldings, in a building specially erected by the 4th Marquess of Salisbury, to whom her father, George Norman, had been Head Gardener in the 1880s and '90s.

36 Upper Handside Farm had an impressive array of barns when this photograph was taken in *c.*1920. In 1932 barns and farmhouse were pulled down as the new Welwyn Garden City began to grow. Only the carthouse, seen in the centre, survives today as the Edward Backhouse Memorial Room in Handside Lane. The Horn family had farmed here since the 1830s and later took over the nearby Lower Handside Farm (now the Barn Theatre) and Brickwall Farm, near Lemsford (now a nursing home). Handside dates back as a farm to at least the 16th century and was farmed by the Battell family (who also had farms within the parish at Stanborough and Woodside), the Tharps and the wealthy Fearnley-Whittingstall's before *c.*1835.

37 The river Lea below Lemsford Mill in *c.*1900 when the main road still passed through the village and up the hill beside the wall of Brocket Park to Brickwall, Ayot and Welwyn. The old cottage (centre background) is the original beerhouse and bakery of James William Smith, best known as the *Long & Short Arm* public house, with its four distinctive dormer windows. It was demolished in the mid-1930s and the present public house was built on the site. The Wesleyan Chapel and cottages to its right have also been demolished, but the cottage to its rear still remains. The *Sun* public house was the home of the Gilbert family in 1718 and an 'alehouse', but from the 1830s to the late 1930s was run by the Allen and then the Halsey families. Just out of the photograph (lower right), it remains to this day.

38 St John's at Lemsford was built in 1858 by the Dowager Countess Cowper as a memorial to her husband, the 6th Earl Cowper, who died in 1856. The architect was David Brandon who was responsible for the reconstruction of St Etheldreda's in 1871. Lemsford was made an ecclesiastical parish in 1859. This photograph was taken before the addition of the Brocket Chapel to the south side of the chancel in 1930 by the architect F.E. Howard.

39 Lemsford Mill was on the site of an earlier mill dating back to Domesday. It was rebuilt in 1863 and worked until *c.*1905, after which it became a light engineering works. This photograph dates to the 1960s or '70s. Converted to offices in the 1980s, it was given a Civic Trust award in 1986. Its main claim to fame is that it is the 'Old Mill by the Stream' in the Nelly Dean song popular with soldiers of the Boer War who were billeted in the village.

40 Lemsford village post office opened *c.*1889 under the charge of James Wilmot, boot and shoe maker, whose sign hangs over the door in this photograph of *c.*1910. His daughter Cissie stands in the doorway. Before it was opened, letters went through Welwyn post office. Following its closure in the early 1930s, the post office moved to the Lemsford General Stores near the Mill. This was enlarged and rebuilt in 1937 with a small café above. The building to the left of the post office is the former Wesleyan chapel, closed in *c.*1930 and used by the Wilmots as a store and workshop. None of these buildings now survive and the site is a car park for the *Long & Short Arm* public house.

41 The *Bull* public house, Stanborough has been renamed and resited many times in a history which dates back at least to the 18th century. The building, seen here in a rare photograph published in Frank King's book *The Story of the Canon Brewery 1751-1951*, was on the corner of what is now Brocket Road and the Great North Road, opposite to the modern public house built in the 1930s, which is now a Steakhouse restaurant.

42 The Great North Road, known at the time as plain North Road, looking north at Brickwall Hill 1919 or 1920. The road to Lemsford village was on the left; to the right at the bottom of Tinker's Hill were two early 20th-century estate cottages demolished when this section of the A1 was upgraded to motorway in the late 1960s. The white building, on the corner of what was soon to become Valley Road, was an Enquiry Office for Welwyn Garden City Ltd., developers of the new town.

43 The *Chequers* at Cromer Hyde, Lemsford has been a pub or beerhouse since at least 1750. Before that it was a small manor house or farm known as Hornby or Hornbeam Hall on the Brocket estate, and for a time appears to have served a dual function. In the 1880s it was owned by Searancke's brewery in Hatfield, then by Pryor Reid's Hatfield Brewery before becoming a Benskins (Watford) house in the mid-1920s. Local hunts were a regular sight there between the wars. Only since 1970 has the pub taken its present name of the *Crooked Chimney*. This is one of up to six pubs in the village since the 1840s including the *Sun* (or *Rising Sun*); *The Roebuck* (near the Mill) the *Waggon and Horses* (nearly opposite the church); the *Angel* (Brickwall Hill, demolished 1850) and the *Long & Short Arm*.

44 The former turnpike toll-house, Mount Pleasant, near Oldings Corner, Great North Road, erected by the Galley Corner Turnpike Trust. Formed in 1730, this Trust took over the responsibility for maintaining the road from Galley Corner, near Barnet, to Lemsford Mill in the north of Hatfield parish. Behind is Warren Lodge, farmed in the 20th century by Richard Horsey. The buildings were demolished in the 1960s. Stables now occupy the site, which is close to the modern Tesco superstore.

45 Until the extension of the Barnet By-pass to Hatfield in 1926-7, the Great North Road ran over the railway via Wrestlers Bridge and down past the old Turnpike Gate at Mount Pleasant to Stanborough. Since the 1730s travellers have been able to pause for refreshment at the *Wrestlers* (or *Two Wrestlers*) public house, seen here. The building was unusual in having no beer cellars, retaining instead an outhouse kept cool by an earth bank. In 1966-7 the building was extensively altered and little of the original now remains. This coincided with the collapse of nearby Wrestlers Bridge in 1966, which was never rebuilt for vehicular traffic, leaving the pub in a cul-de-sac. In time this proved an asset not the disaster anticipated immediately afterwards.

46 The water corn mill at Mill Green, Hatfield, had served the town as its manorial mill for some 900 years when its last miller, Sidney Christmas Lawrance, ceased milling in 1911. The present structure was extensively rebuilt and extended in 1762 when the Bigg family were millers, but other buildings on the site are much older. When the mill ceased operating, the wooden waterwheel, with iron buckets, and machinery were still intact. Restoration of the mill was begun in 1973 by the Hatfield and District Archaeological Society. This work was taken over in 1979 in a partnership between the Mill Green Water Mill Restoration Trust and the District Council. After several years of careful restoration, the machinery was restored to working order, the waterwheel completely rebuilt (the old one being too decayed) and the first flour milled again in 1986. The Mill and adjoining District Museum (opened 1978) are now open all year round.

47 The *Crooked Billet*, Mill Green. First mentioned in 1773 when owned by Searancke, later becoming part of Hatfield Brewery property. Three members of the Russell family lived there for half a century, to within a few months of its closure, by Benskins, in 1936, to provide a licence for *The Comet* on the Barnet Bypass, Hatfield. The old pub was demolished. Its close neighbour, *The Green Man*, is still trading.

48 Mrs. Helen Toms outside her shop in Roe Green Lane (now College Lane), Hatfield, *c*.1932. By the gate (*left to right*): Sonia Toms, Renee Willett and Philip Toms.

49 The Roe Green 'Iron Room' or Mission Room, the gift of the 3rd Marchioness of Salisbury, was opened on 23 December 1888. In 1953 a sanctuary and vestry were added and the whole 'tin church' dedicated in the name of St John. Services transferred to the Cavendish Hall in 1955. In 1960 the new church of St John, built at the highest point in the New Town on a site given by the 5th Marquess of Salisbury, was consecrated. The old Mission Room was used for religious services by the Brethren from 1957. It continued in use by the community for whist drives, wedding receptions, Women's Institute and cycle club meetings. By the 1980s it was in a poor state of repair. It was demolished in September 1994.

50 The original mission room at Chiswell Green was built in 1890 for the people living in Cooper's Green, Astwick, Symondshyde and elsewhere. It was designed by Mr. Shillito and built by Mr. W. Richardson. It could seat 60 and was used once a week for a Sunday School followed by Evensong. After only eight years it had fallen into disrepair and had to be demolished. The photograph shows the building which Lord Salisbury donated in its place. This was timber like the first structure. It continued in use until the 1930s. It was requisitioned during the Second World War and later demolished.

51 St Mary Magdalene's Church at Hatfield Hyde was built by Lord Salisbury in 1882 to replace the so-called 'mud chapel' nearby, used since 1861 as a place of worship and later as the village school. Designed by Eustace Balfour (a nephew of the 3rd Marquess), it opened for worship on 22 July 1883. Much of the interior woodwork, notably the reredos, was carved by H.J.B. Kendall of nearby Hyde House. A fine modern brass to the Kendall family can be seen near the north door. This photograph shows the church before it was extended in 1957, by which time Hatfield Hyde had been a separate parish for 30 years and was serving the needs of growing Welwyn Garden City.

52 Hatfield Hyde did not become a separate parish until 1927, but had its present church of St Mary Magdalene, opened in 1882, and its first purpose-built school, established in 1875. This photograph, taken outside the school, *c*.1898, shows the 13 boys and 18 girls of Class I, many in the leather boots common in agricultural areas. At this time the school had six Managers, with Mrs. Georgiana Kendall of nearby Hyde House as 'Correspondent'. The rather plain school building, supported with brick buttresses and with its bell turret in the centre, closed in 1932, became a furniture store, and was later destroyed by fire. Only the school bell was saved. One former pupil wrote 'Discipline was very strict ... the cane was kept in a locked cupboard in the headmistress' room ... it often came out!'

53 The *Beehive* is one of the oldest buildings in Hatfield Hyde, now part of Welwyn Garden City. It is first recorded as being licensed in 1842. By 1850 William Higgs was the under-tenant of Peter McMullen, a member of the Hertford brewing family. Higgs also traded as a grocer from the premises. The pub is now run as a Beefeater restaurant. This postcard was published for Welwyn Stores (1929) Ltd. by the Photochrom Co. Ltd.

54 The once picturesque row of 10 Victorian terrace houses, known as Sandpit or Gravel Pit Cottages, once stood on the corner of Woodhall Lane and Hollybush Lane, Hatfield Hyde. They were built for workers at Smart's Sand and Gravel works, situated near Twentieth Mile Bridge and Woodhall Lodge Farm. Before the First World War no.1 was a sub-post office run by Mrs. Welch. Today the site, opposite the Family Centre of Our Lady's Roman Catholic Church, is occupied by flats. Sandpit Cottages, together with others like 'The Row' near the former *Woodman* public house, were demolished to make way for the new Welwyn Garden City as it 'submerged' the old village of Hatfield Hyde.

55 The east side of Hunter's Bridge, Welwyn Garden City, named after the Hunter family, tenants of Pear Tree Farm, photographed by F. Mayo of Oaklands, Welwyn in 1926. The cottages on the right-hand side have been demolished. In the distance is Welwyn Garden City halt. Hunter's Bridge was part of Hatfield parish until 1921 when the new parish of Welwyn Garden City was established.

56 A modern house now stands on the site of the blacksmith's shop in Bell Bar, an old-established hamlet now off the beaten track but originally on the through route of the road from London to the north of England. The new Great North Road by-passed Bell Bar in the mid-19th century. At this time the hamlet had three inns, several farms, a bakery, a wheelwright's and a blacksmith's. The blacksmith's was owned by Robert Gaussen and occupied by William Bamford. It was demolished in the 1950s or '60s some time after this postcard was produced by Photomatic of Welham Green.

57 Little is known about the Children's Home in Newgate Street, seen here in a postcard of *c.*1908, but a school was built in the village in 1847 at the same time as the church. Newgate Street was segregated from Hatfield parish to form a separate ecclesiastical parish in 1912.

58 The *Crown* at Newgate Street dates as a pub from at least 1811 and by the 1870s had a smithy attached. This photograph was taken some thirty years before the building was demolished in 1938 and the present one erected. As the signboard on the wall indicates, it was owned at the time by Christie & Co., the Hoddesdon brewery. Another notice to its left advertises 'Teas', probably catering for the many weekend cyclists then on the roads. The village pump stood opposite the inn.

59 The *Woodman* at Wildhill was owned by the Marquess of Salisbury. It is first recorded in 1851 when it was leased to Complin's Brewery. Afterwards it was leased to Hatfield and Benskins breweries. The original pub, now demolished, stood a little to the east of this building to which the licence was transferred in the late 19th century. Since 1964 the *Woodman* has been a free house.

60 A ceremonial archway erected at the lower end of Fore Street between the *Eight Bells* and *One Bell* public houses, to celebrate a visit by Queen Victoria and Prince Albert to Hatfield House from 22 to 24 October 1846. The royal carriage was accompanied from Watford to Hatfield by an escort of the South Hertfordshire Yeomanry Cavalry who remained at Hatfield House during the two-day visit. A ball was given by the 3rd Marquess and Marchioness on 23 October for their royal visitors, but neither the Queen nor Prince Albert reportedly made a very good impression on the assembled guests.

61 Hatfield's Market House stood at the lower end of Fore Street in 1607, where it is shown on a map of that date. In the 17th century the town's official weights and measures were probably kept there, and occasional courts were held there. The market place and stalls were set up around it and in the street. The narrowness of Fore Street at this point, plus increased wheeled traffic trying to pass, led to the re-routing of the road and the removal of the Market House and market to the site shown in this drawing of 1832 by J.C. Buckler. The move took place in the 1760s and by the 1830s the upper floor was used as a school for a short time. In *c*.1850 the building was finally demolished and another historic link with the past lost.

62 A drawing by Caroline Faithfull (daughter of the Rev. F.J. Faithfull, Rector of Hatfield 1819-54) of the new National School on London Road. Built and furnished by public subscription in 1850, with a teacher's house attached, it first housed infants and girls and, when extended in 1854, boys as well. Within fifty years it was too small for all the classes and in 1905 a separate boys' school was built in Endymion Road. By 1913, only girls were left at London Road, moving to the St Audrey's site in 1924, where the school remained until 1957. Countess Anne School now occupies most of the Endymion Road site. The London Road building, together with Gray's and Water's garages almost opposite, were demolished in the 1960s.

63 George Lawrence, known locally as 'Cock o' me Dandy', was Hatfield's last town crier when he died in 1910 at the age of seventy-four. He was buried in St Luke's churchyard on 11 May. One of his last duties was to proclaim the visit to Hatfield House of King Edward VII and Queen Alexandra in the year before his death. Seen here with the traditional handbell and notice, he was the last representative locally of a tradition going back several centuries.

64 The old town *en fête* in 1909 where London Road meets Broadway. On the left is the *Dray Horse* public house and refreshment rooms, by then a popular stopping place for cyclists. Only 12 years earlier the parish council was seeking permission to erect notices requesting cyclists to 'ride slowly through this town', adding that 'The Police have orders to prosecute any cyclist riding so as to endanger the public safety'. Next on the left the *Salisbury Arms Temperance Hotel*, on the corner of Cage Hill and London Road (opened 1885), with its fine brick chimneys and its proprietor, Hugh Harvey, promoting the hotel's restaurant, tea room, billiard and games rooms, meeting rooms etc. with blatant signboarding.

65 Motorists entering Hatfield by the London Road in the early years of this century were doubtless gratified to find two thriving motor businesses side by side. First was Walter Waters' recently acquired premises where he and his two sons built, serviced and sold cars, motorcycles and bicycles. Next door was pioneer motor engineer James Gray (d.1913), whose coach building and motor works included spacious first-floor showrooms for their products, many built to order. Mr. Gray was also chief of the Hatfield Volunteer Fire Brigade and its 40 h.p. towing engine was stored at his premises shortly before this photograph was taken, *c*.1908. Both businesses continue to trade in Hatfield to the present day on different sites, the buildings shown in the photograph having been demolished. In the left foreground is the National (London Road) School, opened in 1850.

66 Gray's Motor Works developed from a small wheelwright's shop established on the new London Road in the early 1850s by Ebenezer Bunker. James Gray took over the business, which included coach-building, in 1882. In 1886 he pulled down the old shops and put up a new building which he extended twice during the next decade. By this time all types of motor and carriage bodies were being manufactured. After his death in 1913, Jimmy Gray was succeeded by his two sons. In 1945 the business was sold to the Clark family who traded under the old name. Following the re-routing of the Great North Road and re-development of Old Hatfield, the garage was re-located to the western side of the road. In 1994 the company was purchased by Diamond Rover.

67 March past Hatfield Brewery, owned by the Pryor family and then by Pryor, Reid & Co. Ltd. from the 1830s until 1920. The photograph dates to *c*.1910, but what event or ceremony was taking place is not known. The band is thought to be that of the Hertfordshire Regiment. The main interest is that it shows some of the main brewery buildings, the manager's house and a sign on the right for the main office.

68 A Hatfield Brewery motorised dray of *c*.1914 with uniformed driver. The Pryor family of Baldock acquired the brewery in Hatfield in 1836-7, but it was Alfred Pryor (d.1876) who moved to Hatfield and later became sole owner. Alfred's second son, Edward Vickris Pryor, began the Pryor and Reid family connection in October 1870 when he married Ethel Justina, second daughter of William Reid of The Node, Codicote. Edward bought the Hatfield Brewery soon after his father's death and was joined a few years later by his brother-in-law, Percy Charles Reid. From the 1880s until 1920 Pryor, Reid & Co.'s brewery flourished, taking over A.J. Sherriff's Park Street Brewery and Bradshaw's Newtown Brewery (near where White Lion Square now stands) amongst others. The Brewery even had its own cricket team. When P.C. Reid's only son, Lt. Geoffrey Reid, was killed in action in 1915, there was nobody to take over the business and it was forced to close in March 1920 and was sold to Benskin's of Watford.

69 Brewery Hill was so-called because of the Pryor, Reid Brewery which closed in 1920. In the background is St Etheldreda's with its spire which was taken down in 1930. On the right of centre is the *Dray Horse*, to its left hand side the *One Bell* public house, between them extensive stables. The new Salisbury Square now occupies the site.

70 Looking north up Brewery Hill in May 1961 shortly before extensive demolition of parts of the old town began. On the left P.V. Patemen, grocers. Next with the sun blind saying 'Hatfield Fruit Stores' is P.J. Stagden, greengrocers; then H.W. Walby's, butchers and J. Busby, chemist. Past the Westminster Bank (Manager, the late E.G. Copus), W. Smith, fishmonger; the International (Tea Co.) Stores and Dewhurst the butcher. On the bend, past the trees, the surgery of Dr. L. Burvill-Holmes. On the right, W. Water's Garage, T. Butler, butchers, Simmons the Bakers, Park Café and Mervyn Powell, photographer. Just out of the photograph are A.A. Dollimore, greengrocers and Drury Bros., outfitters.

71 Brewery Hill, the Great North Road, October 1967. Shops include the old town branches of Simmons and Busby's the Chemist. Only the buildings on the right-hand side of Brewery Hill now survive as part of the modern Salisbury Square.

72 The *Eight Bells*, formerly the *Five Bells*, on the corner of Park Street and Fore Street. Charles Dickens, who came to Hatfield as a newspaper reporter to cover the fire which killed the 1st Marchioness of Salisbury, included it in *Oliver Twist*. The book's villain, Bill Sykes, calls there for a drink following his murder of Nancy. Since this photograph was taken by the postcard company Valentine in the early 1900s, the pub has taken over the adjoining shop premises.

73 Fore Street was once the main road through the town after it left Hatfield Park. This notably traffic-free photograph of *c*.1912 shows (*left*) the office of the National Telephone Company (shortly afterwards Post Office Telephones' exchange and public call office); Hankin's drapers shop; Henry Hill the baker and Sidney Christmas Lawrance's cycle shop. At the top of the street, the *East India Chief* and the gateway to Hatfield House. The lady on the right is passing James Cox ('Doc Cox' as he was known) the chemist and druggist and Pettit & Co, high class grocers (*see* Plate 74). The boy with the wheelbarrow in the middle of the road is collecting horse droppings.

74 Fore Street once had a market at its lower end, but by the time this photograph was taken in *c*.1912 it was a mixture of shops and private houses. On the right can be seen the shops of John Thomas, baker (run at this date by his widow Rebecca and later by their children), with next door Arthur Edmund Sharp's extensive drapers business. Adjoining Sharp's was the well-remembered chemist and druggist James 'Doc' Cox, who frequently dispensed to the poor unable to pay for a doctor to call. The three shops were created out of the former and extensive *Kings Head Inn*, renamed Waterloo House, *c*.1815. There was a saddlers next to Cox's for many years and the low building next to that was, from *c*.1750 to *c*.1930, a grocers, including from *c*.1898 the high class business of Pettit & Co, 'grocers and ironmongers'.

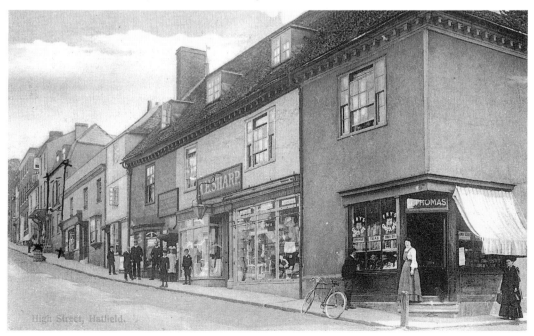

75 A Frith postcard from the top of Fore Street in the 1940s or early '50s. On the left-hand side can be seen the entrance to St Etheldreda's Church. Opposite is the *East Indian Chief* public house. This was known as the *Roebuck* alias the *Nags Head* in 1776. Shortly after, in 1789, it became the *Marquis of Granby*. In the early 1850s it was known as the *Full Measure*, assuming the name *East Indian Chief* by 1855. It is now a private house.

76 Some of the buildings of Georgian Hatfield still survive at the top of Fore Street, but the Georgian cafe has closed since this photograph was taken in October 1967 and many more parked cars now line the street. Thanks to the 'improvements' carried out in the 1920s and '30s by the antique dealer, F.W. Speaight, it is not clear how many of the doorways are original to the houses. There were several pubs and shops here in the 1780s, including Edmund Long, the baker; Thomas Wickes the Peruke (wig) maker and the *Roebuck* or *Nags Head*.

77 Park Street (formerly Duck Lane) looking south towards Fore Street, *c.*1906. On the left Fenning Brothers, grocers (who left in 1908 when it became Hammond & Co, also a grocers); Ralph Humphrey's printing shop opened in 1905 in what had been the *Jacob's Well* since 1850, a public house of some notoriety; past the passage leading to Park Street Chapel the *Butchers Arms*, closed *c.*1909 but remaining as a butcher's shop until 1955. On the right the *Horse & Groom* remains to this day, and next door the double-gabled front of the Old Coach House, originally a hall house, with cross wing, of *c.*1500.

78 Park Street looking north *c.*1909-10 when it was a thriving series of small shops and businesses. No.1, on the left, Thomas Gregory's china and glass shop (and local agents for Goss Crested China) is not visible, but some of Hankin & Sons, drapers, outfitters and 'boot factors', can be seen. Next door was the Old Coach House, part of which was a baker's shop from the mid-18th century. Its owner, E. S. Jesshop, blatantly promotes Hovis bread as well as his own 'Wedding & Birthday Cakes'. Beyond this the *Horse & Groom* and Walby's butcher's shop on the corner of Arm & Sword Yard. On the right the sign of Harry Burgess' boot and shoe shop, its sign ending 'Repairs Neatly Executed'. He had moved from Arm & Sword Yard shortly before.

79 Arthur Charles Osborn ran his fruiterer's and fishmonger's business in Park Street from the 1920s until the mid-1930s. Seen here outside his shop at nos. 3 and 5, his delivery van proudly displays 'Best Quality' fish and poultry. Sadly his shop did not survive competition from other traders. The premises were later to become part of the very first shop opened by Sidney Rumbelow, the founder of what later was to become a national chain of radio and television retailers. Sid Rumbelow himself was also an accomplished musician.

80 H.W. Walby & Son's butcher's shop on the corner of Park Street and Arm & Sword Yard, *c.*1928. Henry William Walby died in 1925 and the business was taken over by his son Joseph Canham Walby (d.1974) seen here in the centre with his staff. (*Left to right*): Tommy Barrett; Sidney Hart; J.C. Walby; George 'Razor' Hill; unidentified. This shop moved to another site on the former Great North Road in 1935 and later to its present site in the new Salisbury Square.

81 One of the few known views of Arm & Sword Yard, off Park Street, known locally as 'Blood & Gut Alley' when at least one slaughterhouse opened on to it. Nineteenth-century censuses record a large number of families living here, the women and young girls working as straw plaiters and hat makers. The first building on the left is where Alfred Dollimore began his greengrocer's business soon after the First World War (in which he won the Military Cross), and which remained in Hatfield until some ten years ago. Henry Boswell, one of his employees, stands in the doorway. On the lower right side is the back of H.W. Walby's butchers shop (*see* plate 80). At the top of the street, on the left, stood Priory House, now demolished, and on the right the *Great Northern Hotel* (now the *Hatfield Arms*). All the other buildings have been demolished and most of the site is a car park.

82 Arthur Edmund Sharp (1852-1910) opened his draper's shop at 23 Fore Street in 1876, taking over his nephew Mark Powell's linen draper's business when the latter died. Later Mr. Sharp extended both the premises, through to Church Street as seen in the photograph, and the range of goods on sale. By 1907 the latest French and English millinery could be bought, in a selection equal to many London shops. Before the buildings were demolished in the 1960s, they contained the stationer's shop run by the late (Lillian) Daisy Gray (died 1984). At the end of the alleyway can be seen the *Eight Bells* public house.

83 Church Street in October 1967. On the left is E.G. Hart's grocer's shop which provided a mobile shop serving Welham Green. The premises are now occupied by Simmons the Bakers. The old lock-up or cage was sited where the corner shop now stands, seen here on the right.

84 The *Baker's Arms* in Church Street, *c.*1925 when Ernest E. Peters was licensee. The pub took its name from the trade of its first owners, the Bradshaw family, who ran a baker's shop in conjunction with their beerhouse from the 1850s. They also owned Newtown Brewery. The pub became a Pryor Reid & Co's house in the 1890s, and by the time of its closure in 1928 had been a Benskin's house for some three years. Another pub, the *Two Brewers*, stood opposite until 1886 when it was demolished and St Audrey's built as the Rectory.

85 Church Cottage with part of the former *Bakers Arms* behind, photographed on 7 March 1989. In the 1850s the *Bakers Arms* was kept by the Bradshaw family, former bakers and owners of the Newtown Brewery. It closed in 1928. Both buildings were skilfully restored by the local antique dealer F.W. Speaight, who lived in Hatfield between about 1910 and 1930. Church Cottage has been used as the residence of successive senior curates at the parish church since the 1920s.

86 The late Jack Flegg's garden at no.8 Church Street in Hatfield became as much a part of the local history of the town as Jack himself. Known affectionately as 'Mr Local History', his interest and knowledge of Old Hatfield was legendary. He lived in the town for almost fifty years, having worked for many of them at the former International Stores in North Road. He began model making in *c.*1964 and displayed his work in his small, colourful garden. Several models were of local buildings like that of the *Eight Bells* in the photograph; others had personal associations. Since he died on 9 January 1994, one of his models has gone to the Victoria & Albert Museum; others are in the local Mill Green Museum. Lord Salisbury allowed his funeral cortège to drive through Hatfield Park as a special mark of respect.

87 Built on the site of the Old Workhouse Yard between 1850 and *c.*1853, the double terrace of cottages in Salisbury Square, erected by the 2nd Marquess of Salisbury (d.1868), housed the Sergeants of the Permanent Staff of the Hartfordshire Militia. A Band Room was also added in 1854, together with an armoury nearby. Hatfield became the headquarters of the Harts Militia from 1853-73, then returning to Hertford. By 1861 the cottages housed a quartermaster and his wife and 16 sergeants and their families (68 persons in total), plus eight drummer boys. Ten years later there were only seven sergeants in residence, but 37 family members (of which 28 were children), plus 10 drummer boys, and within two years they too had gone. For their last 100 years, until demolished in 1972, the cottages were rented out by the Salisbury Estate, a communal pump providing water for several decades. To their rear can be seen the 29 steps known locally as 'Jacob's Ladder', leading to and from Church Street.

88 The Park Street Chapel was the first to be built in Hatfield for Nonconformist worship. Completed in 1823, it has been described as 'small but simple and dignified'. In 1925 the chapel was first described as the Congregational Church of Hatfield. A new church, Christ Church, was opened in Newtown in 1932. Sadly, the old chapel was demolished in the 1960s and the graveyard was destroyed. A few of the gravestones survive to the rear of the houses now on the site.

89 The Wesleyan Methodist Church in French Horn Lane opened on 30 October 1889. Designed by Mr. E. Hoote, it was built on the site of half of a pair of villas at a cost of £2,000 including £800 for the land—a large sum of money at the time. The church closed for worship in April 1938, when a new church in Birchwood Avenue was opened, and the building sold was to E. T. Tingey & Sons as a furniture store. When it was demolished in 1968 to make way for a new railway bridge and roundabout, a silver trowel with ivory handle was found in one of the foundation stones, inscribed: 'Wesleyan Church, Hatfield Memorial Stone laid May 29th 1889 by Mr C. Poulton'.

90 French Horn Lane and Batterdale looking east, *c*.1958. On the right E.T. Tingey's furniture warehouse in the former Wesleyan Chapel and, beyond the end buildings, the bell cote of the former London Road School (then K.C.V. Precision Tool Co.). On the left, in Batterdale, part of the fine 18th-century Triangle House, formerly a tanner's house owned by the Walby family, with tan-yard nearby. In the last century it became a doctor's surgery successively for Drs. L. Osbaldeston (d.1897), P.M. Brittain (d.1935) and latterly J.F. O'Neill. Behind it is the tower of St Etheldreda's Church. The advertising hoarding includes a promotion for an Eastern Electricity Board cooker costing 'less than 3d a day to run'! and Colgate's FAB washing powder.

91 The junction of French Horn Lane and Batterdale looking west, *c.*1957, with the iron railway bridge replaced in 1893 and removed in 1970. Beyond the bridge are the still surviving Glebe Cottages and behind Burgess' is the end of one of Hatfield's four signal boxes. J.J. Burgess and Son was founded by James John Burgess senior (1859-1929), a local builder and undertaker. His horse-drawn hearses (two or four horses depending on the job) and hand-drawn bier were a common sight in the town until motorised hearses replaced them. The above premises were demolished after the firm moved to its present premises in The Common in 1969.

92 Howe Dell is now a school, but, beneath the many later alterations and additions to this important house, there is evidence of the earlier timber-framed hall house (some demolished in the late 18th century) and lath and plaster walling. Some interesting early wall painting has been found and there is some good 18th-century plaster ceiling decoration and a fine former stable block of similar date nearby. The house appears to have been the rectory or parsonage from at least the 13th century and until St Audrey's, Church Street was built for the Rev. Lord William Cecil in 1888-9. It became a junior school after the Second World War, although one of the rectory's best known residents, the Rev. Francis J. Faithfull (rector 1819 until his death in 1854), ran a school there for 10-15 boys. Later he built a separate school for girls at the end of his drive, near the old railway bridge over French Horn Lane.

93 St Luke's Church, Newtown, on the St Albans Road was built as a cemetery chapel by the 3rd Marquess of Salisbury in 1877. Regular Sunday services were held from 1888 and an organ was installed the following year. In 1893 the chapel was converted into a cruciform church in the Early English style.

94 Emma and William Vyse in the *Prince of Wales* beerhouse and lodgings, Union Road (now Wellfield Road). This beerhouse was first mentioned in 1867 when it was owned by James Webb. Acquired later in the century by Hatfield Brewery, then by Benskin's, it closed in 1956. This rare interior view dates to *c*.1920. Note the gas lamp over the bar.

95 Looking north towards Tingey's 'Corner Houses' on the St Albans Road in the 1930s. The premises with a tower was a furniture store. Opposite was the firm's ironmongery, china, glass and tools shop. The post office was sited at the Savill's premises from 1931 until 1961 when a purpose-built post office opened in White Lion Square. Ironically, in 1994 it moved back to this part of St Albans Road (now Town Centre).

96 The *Red Lion* inn on the former Great North Road dates from the 18th century, when it came into prominence as one of Hatfield's premier coaching inns. Later it became a Posting House and Revenue Office as well. Even when this photograph was taken in *c*.1905 it still had extensive stabling at the rear. In the 19th century a livestock and corn market was held nearby and property auctions regularly took place there. Cattle pens to the north of the inn were still shown on maps at the turn of the last century. Local businessman Joseph Scarborough ran his coach to and from the *Red Lion* to the *George Inn* at Baldock in the mid-1830s. It served as a licensed hotel from *c*.1890 until 1939. Since the 1950s various extensions have been added, notably the Cranborne Rooms.

97 Two private schools in North Road, known collectively as Hatfield Collegiate Schools, were Dagmar House (boys) and Alexandra House (girls), opened in 1898 and 1900 respectively under their principal John R. Sheehan-Dare. Both had as their pupils children of many prominent local trades and business people, as well as those of families outside the parish. The boys had a flourishing cricket team and an Old Dagmarians football team (founded 1900). Sheehan-Dare remained Principal until 1922-3 when he sold the schools to T.W. Hearle and Mr. and Mrs. J.G. Prentice. The Prentices ran the schools for another 10 years before they finally closed.

98 Girls in the distinctive hats of Alexandra House School on North Road (near Wrestler's Bridge) *c.*1923. This private school, together with Dagmar House School for boys, was owned jointly at this time by Mr. John G. and Mrs. Hilda Prentice, who were also the principals. Its pupils were drawn mainly from Hatfield and other towns and villages within a five-mile radius. Both schools closed about ten years after this photograph was taken.

99 North Road, nearly opposite Hatfield station with (*left to right*) the Hertfordshire Constituency Conservative Association office: the *Great Northern Hotel* (first named the *Douro Arms* until 1859; rebuilt *c.*1900 and now the *Hatfield Arms*); Priory House, a late 17th-century building probably first an inn. It was later owned by Joseph Bigg, who bought Searancke's Brewery for £11,154 in 1815, only to be declared bankrupt four years later! Behind the premises next door was the Public Hall, built by Lord Salisbury in 1910. Here the first silent movies were shown and it also housed the public library until 1950. All the above buildings except the *Hatfield Arms* have now been demolished.

100 Arthur James Sherriff came to Hatfield from Aylesbury in 1872 to take over the lease of Complin's brewery in Park Street with its corn, coal and salt trade. He sold the brewery interests eight years later but retained the corn and coal trade at premises near Hatfield station. Over the years the Sherriff family interests and their trade in corn, fertiliser, feeding stuffs and potatoes expanded. The coal business was dispensed with in 1950. The building shown here was erected in 1899 as a granary. Together with the former fire engine garage, seen here on the right-hand side, it was demolished in 1987 as British Rail wanted the site back for office development.

101 The Sherriffs had other business premises further north on the Great North Road at Burleigh Mead. They purchased land from Lord Salisbury on which they built Hatfield Mill, together with farm cottages, in 1905. These premises had their own railway siding as did the granary by the station. The mill originally had three pairs of stones which were under-driven and used exclusively for grist (milling for animal feed). The original power supply was from a gas engine, the gas being made in an anthracite coking plant behind the mill. Electricity was subsequently installed and the millstones replaced with hammer-mills. These in turn were eventually removed but the building was still used for crop processing and storage. Sherriff's moved to bigger premises at Royston in 1983 and put the site up for sale. Only days before the auction, the Mill was the scene of one of the biggest fires in the town for a decade. Central Ideal Homes Ltd purchased the 2.4 acres of land for £500,000 and built 41 houses. The close's name, Burleigh Mead, preserves the original field name.

102 No.62 Bridge, known locally as Wrestlers' Bridge, was built in 1850 to carry the Great North Road out of Hatfield. On 20 February 1966, as ballast was being excavated from the track during 'blanketing' work, one of the three arches collapsed without warning. Engineers decided to demolish the bridge immediately, during which operation the rest of the structure collapsed, leaving 2,000 tons of rubble on the main line tracks. Gas and water mains were fractured, but a 3,000 core telephone cable, seen in the photograph, was saved. Three days later the lines were re-opened, but the road bridge was never rebuilt and only the present footbridge was put in its place.

103 This early 20th-century view of the original Hatfield station was first published by an Enfield postcard company. Until the station was completely rebuilt in 1972 its old buildings remained mostly intact and included a refreshment and tea room. The 3rd Marquess of Salisbury, who had his own train to take him to and from London, added a private waiting room.

104 Hatfield station opened to passengers of the Great Northern Railway on 7 August 1850 and quickly became an important junction. The goods yard, engine shed and turntable were on the left in this view of *c*.1910. Passengers for the former branch lines to St Albans, Luton & Dunstable and Hertford changed here until the mid-1920s, when Welwyn Garden City station opened and served the latter two lines.

105 A 4-4-0 locomotive No. 4323 on the turntable just north of Hatfield station in 1927. One of the four signal boxes at Hatfield stood to the right just out of the photograph. In the background are some of the Victorian concrete block houses of Beaconsfield Terrace (later Road) now occupied by modern office and business premises.

106 This Metropolitan Electric Company open-topped Daimler bus, with rear staircase, served route 109 between Golders Green station and the *One Bell* public house, Hatfield. Note the solid tyres still then being enforced by the Metropolitan Police on vehicles operating from within their area (which extended, as now, into south Hertfordshire) and the early use of advertising. This photograph was probably taken at Hendon Bus Garage, as Hatfield did not have its own such garage until 1922.

107 The National Omnibus & Transport Company had established a garage in St Albans Road, Hatfield by 1922. In 1925 a bus was running five times a day from Welwyn Garden City through Hatfield to St Albans.

108 A freak hail storm on 8 August 1931 brought widespread damage and flooding to the area. The St Albans to Hatfield and Welwyn Garden City bus is seen here passing under the Hatfield—St Albans branch railway over St Albans Road West.

109 Built in the mid-18th century, and much altered in the early 19th, Goldings (Goldring or Golby) in French Horn Lane was the home of Adolphe Coltier, a Swiss-born teacher of languages, and his family in 1851. From Michaelmas 1856-83 it was leased by Lord Salisbury to Hertfordshire County Police as a police station, until a new County Police Headquarters was opened in St Albans Road. In 1871 the Goldings station was lived in by Inspector Stephen Chapman, his wife and family, and P.C. James Wilson, 'lodger', and there was one prisoner—Francis Randal, a 39-year-old blacksmith. In the photograph, two sergeants and seven other officers, wearing the top hats and frock coats used until 1891, stand in front of the Goldings police station.

110 Hertfordshire County Police Headquarters moved from Hertford to Hatfield in 1883, when the above buildings were opened in St Albans Road. The Chief Constable at the time, Lt. Col. Henry Smith Daniell (1838-1918), ran the force on military lines, even insisting that his men attend church, in uniform, at least once every Sunday! In 1928 the first W.P.C.s, sisters Annie and Margaret Johnson, were appointed; a fingerprint and photographic department opened in 1937 and in 1964 the first regional crime squad operated from Hatfield. The yellow-brick buildings, where occasional courts were held until 1939, remained as County Headquarters until 1967, when a new County Headquarters was opened in Stanborough Road, Welwyn Garden City. Since then the buildings were used variously by Hatfield Parish Council; as a hostel for young homeless known as 'Bridges', and latterly by County Social Services. They were demolished during 1994-5 and redeveloped for housing.

111 Two-way radio communication between Hertfordshire Police headquarters at Hatfield and its patrol cars did not fully materialise until after the Second World War. Much of the pioneering work was done by a local police officer Sergeant S.H.W. ('Doc') Watson (seen here), a major step forward being the building of the once familiar radio mast and communications centre behind the St Albans Road offices. The 'boots' of patrol cars were filled with heavy radio equipment—a far remove from present-day police communications equipment and mobile phones. A VHF multi-carrier radio system was developed later and the first personal pocket radio came into use in November 1965.

112 Hatfield Fire Brigade, *c*.1898. Mr. J. Hollingworth is holding the horses steady. The other men are, from left to right, W.J. Richardson; the driver, G. Warren, W.A. Cornish, Captain T. Christian, George Elliott, B. Pattinson and J.J. Burgess. The spectating boy is T.B. Sharp.

113 Hatfield Fire Brigade members with their new Shand Mason steam pump acquired by the parish council in 1909 and said to be the first of its kind to be used in the county. A 40 h.p. motor vehicle was kept at James Gray's motor works to pull the engine after horses were dispensed with. Fourteen men were in the brigade at this time, including its Captain, Tom Christian, Lieutenant James Gray, John Andrews (engineer), J.J. Burgess (builder and undertaker) and W.J. Richardson (builder), all with over 20 or 25 years' service as volunteer firemen.

114 The Engine House in Batterdale was built by J. Nash for Hatfield Parish Council in 1899, to house the brigade's manual fire engine and hoses. From 1900 the volunteer firemen were also paid a small 'retainer' for the first time. Their Captain was Thomas Christian (who helped form the brigade in 1881) and its Lieutenant James Gray. Christian was also Manager at Pryor Reid's Brewery nearby, where there was a major fire in May 1908 attended by the Hatfield, Hatfield House (Capt. J. Pateman) and St Albans Brigades. The Batterdale station remained in use until January 1966 after which it was demolished and the present fire station in Wellfield Road was opened.

115 Hatfield has had a designated post office since the late 18th century, when the *White Lion Inn*, Fore Street (later named the *Salisbury Arms*) was chosen. After two other sites in Fore Street, the Dunham family moved the post office to a premises adjoining what shortly afterwards became the *Salisbury Temperance Hotel*, London Road. It remained there until May 1936 when the General Post Office opened the post office shown in this photograph opposite the railway station. The official opening was carried out by Lord Salisbury. The builder was J. Honour & Sons of Tring, Hertfordshire and the premises included a new automatic telephone exchange. It closed as a post office in November 1961, when a new post office and sorting office opened in White Lion Square.

116 Dr. Lovell Drage (1858-1919) and his driver Edward George Walby (1879-1962) outside North Place on North Road, *c.*1898. Dr. Drage was the son of the famous Dr. Charles Drage of North Place (d.1922), known as a courteous, no-nonsense physician of the 'old school', who often prescribed wine or spirit instead of medicine. Charles Drage largely attended the rich and included prime ministers Palmerston, Melbourne and Salisbury amongst his patients. Lovell Drage joined his father at Hatfield in 1885 and held a number of public appointments, including medical officer to the Union Workhouse and to the Hatfield Rural District Council, as well as Coroner for the St Albans Division and Staff Surgeon to the Hertfordshire Constabulary. He lived at Burleigh Mead, almost opposite Dagmar House School in North Road.

Opening
of the
New Post Office,
Hatfield, Herts
Monday, 25th May, 1936

117 (*right*) With the First World War about to begin, this recruiting march past in July 1914 appears to include both local defence volunteers (in civvies) and regular officers and NCOs of the Yeomanry or Territorial Forces. Behind them can be seen members of the Boy Scouts and of Hatfield Fire Brigade. It is not clear who is on the dais in front of the *Dray Horse* public house as the march past enters Broadway from London Road. Of over 800 men from the town who joined the services, and whose names were recorded in a special Book of Remembrance and Roll of Honour given to each family or man concerned by Lord and Lady Salisbury, 141 died.

118 (*below*) Sunshine and shadow as troops of the 20th London Regiment march down North Road to Hatfield station in 1915. Troops were billeted throughout the town and few families could refuse to house them. Their departure is watched by local people, many wearing fashionable straw boaters; note also the prominent bill board on the stable wall advertising F.W. Speaight's Hatfield Gallery of Antiques in Goodrich House, Fore Street.

119 (*below*) Troops billeted at the Workhouse, Union Lane, later Wellfield Road, during the First World War. The site of the first known workhouse at Hatfield was on land south of where the *Salisbury Hotel* now stands, below Church Street in Old Hatfield. In 1789 a new Workhouse was erected on Stockbridge Common, then a considerable distance away from the town. It is not known why this happened. Possible reasons include the need for larger accommodation and the objection of residents to a workhouse in central Hatfield. The old premises held 60 inmates, the new more than double that number. They were employed growing food, manufacturing silk and plaiting straw for hat making. By the end of the 19th century vagrants had largely replaced parish paupers. The building closed as a workhouse in 1929 and it became a home and hospital for the elderly. The last residents were transferred to Hertford prior to its demolition in 1989.

120 The headmaster (J.R. Sheehan-Dare) and boys of Dagmar House School constructing a 'bomb-proof dug out' behind the school in North Road in October 1915. It was being built to protect the staff and children there, and at the adjoining Alexandra House School for girls, following a Zeppelin bombing at Hertford shortly before in which nine people had died. A note under the photograph says the shelter was 'passed by the Military Authorities on November 6th 1915 as A1'.

121 Some of the earliest tank trials of the First World War took place in Hatfield Park on 29 January 1916. Known as 'Mother', this 31-ft., 18-ton armoured vehicle was tested over a specially prepared course, and in great secrecy, at the instigation of Winston Churchill. In its second trial on 2 February, 'Mother' crossed a 9 ft. trench, and again a few days later during a private demonstration attended by King George V, by which time the makers, Messrs. Foster of Lincoln, had made six machines. By the time the Battle of the Somme began in September 1916 many more had been made, although Kitchener dismissed the prototype at Hatfield as 'a pretty mechanical toy ...!'

122 'Northcotts' in North Road, between the former post office (*see* plate 115) and North Place, was opened as a military (V.A.D.) hospital on 1 June 1916 by the Hatfield Red Cross and Comforts Committee. Staffed by volunteers, it ran largely on donations and gifts of food. The Commandant was Mrs. Gwendoline R. Bennett of Garden House, Fore Street (the daughter of John S. Lloyd of Astwick Manor, Hatfield), whose husband J.W.M. Bennett, was Hon. Treasurer of the above committee. The figure in the centre is Dr. Lovell Drage (d.1919) in characteristic bow tie. By the time the hospital closed on Friday, 7 February 1919 some 790 patients had been treated there.

123 During the First World War, Waters Garage on the London Road was taken over for munitions manufacture. In this photograph, taken on 16 November 1918, the women display shell cases and tongs. The church on the left-hand side of the picture is the Wesleyan Chapel opened in 1889. It was in use up to 1938 when it was sold to Tingey and Son for a furniture store. It was demolished in the late 1960s.

124 This view looking northwards along the Barnet By-pass was taken in the early 1930s prior to the building of the *Comet Hotel* and shows clearly how undeveloped Hatfield was at this time. Note the St Albans branch railway (closed to passengers in 1951 but used for freight to Smallford until 1969) running diagonally across the picture.

125 The Barnet By-pass, part of the A1, was built in 1927 to divert through-traffic from the Great North Road. The *Stone House Hotel*, here called the new garage, was a familiar landmark before its demolition prior to the construction of the cut-and-cover scheme, 1984 to 1986. Note the Royal Automobile Club box on the junction and the site of de Havilland's Aircraft factory on the left.

126 The administration and design block, constructed for de Havilland's Aircraft Company in the 1930s, is now a listed building. The design department moved into purpose-built accommodation in the 1950s. This is currently in use by the Art and Design department of the University of Hertfordshire. The road, Comet Way, the former Barnet By-pass, has encroached onto the site, but the ornamental pool still survives.

127 Aerial view of the aerodrome taken in June 1935. The facilities of the London Aeroplane Club included a club house and restaurant, tennis courts and a swimming pool. The apprentices from the aircraft factory were allowed to use it immediately before the water was changed. The factory, just off the foreground of the picture, was already very extensive. The buildings with the pitched roofs are the aerodrome's service department with lock-ups beyond. To their right, in isolation, are the petrol pumps. The attractive glass beacon is now preserved at the Mosquito Museum, Salisbury Hall.

128 Originally called the Clock House, the Stone House on the Barnet By-pass was (partly) designed and built in 1933 by the motor engineers W.G. and F.N. Waters who also opened a garage next door. It was acquired by Charrington & Co. in the 1950s. This well-known Hatfield landmark was demolished during the building of the 'cut-and-cover' scheme for the A1(M) in the first half of the 1980s.

129 The shape of the *Comet Hotel* was inspired by the famous red de Havilland 88 Comet Racer No. 34 'Grosvenor House', flown at world record speed from London to Melbourne in 1934 by C.W.A. Scott and T.C. Black in 70 hours 54 minutes and 18 seconds. The building was designed by architect E. B. Musman (1888-1972) for Benskins (Watford) Brewery Ltd. and opened at Christmas 1936. Also of interest is the carved stone pylon, designed and engraved by Eric Kennington, illustrating 18 methods of flight and surmounted by a red model of the Comet Racer, with a comet (or shooting star) passing beneath it. The original model seen here was replaced in 1970 and its successor was restored in 1994 to mark the 60th anniversary of the event.

130 The Birchwood area of Hatfield began growing rapidly in the 1930s and in 1937 a temporary wooden church was erected in Birchwood Avenue dedicated to St Michael and All Angels. After the Second World War, local parishioners built a second, prefabricated church near the *Hopfields* public house, dedicated in November 1946. The present brick church of St Michael's on the same site, with its Romanesque-like east end, was designed by N.F. Cachemaille-Day and consecrated on 9 July 1955 by the Bishop of St Albans.

131 Dagmar House School football team, 1922, outside the school in North Road. Included in the photograph are the school's principal (*left*), John R. Sheehan-Dare; music master, church organist and choirmaster, Harold W. Harrison (*right*) and local boys C.J. 'Kipper' Smith, later a fishmonger in Pond Hill (*middle row, second from left*); Randall J. Tingey, who took over the family grocer's business in Newtown (*middle row, fourth from left*) and (*front row, centre and right*) J.G. Dunham (later licensee of *Great Northern Hotel*, now the *Hatfield Arms*) and Robert 'Bob' Canham (later licensee of *The Gun* public house in Newtown).

132 Hatfield United Football Club (founded in 1901) was one of 10 participants joining the revived Hertfordshire County League in 1935. The 1935-6 season proved a memorable one, for Hatfield's First XI was to win the County League Championship Shield (*seen above*) and the Bingham-Cox Cup and Welwyn Hospital Cup in 1936. In the next season, 1936-7, the first team were runners-up in the County League, but won the Bingham-Cox Cup again. Pictured here (*left to right, back row*) are Harry Tomlin, Harold Bray, Fred Cracknell, Cyril Clayden, Cyril Holton, Ralph England, Bert Nicholas; (*left to right, front row*) Stan Watson, Bob Childs, William H. Warner, William 'Jock' McCrone (Captain), Joe Platts, Ray Evans and Fred Tyler.

133 The once familiar clock tower and entrance to Jack Olding's factory at the junction of the A1 and Mount Pleasant Lane decorated to celebrate the coronation of Queen Elizabeth II in 1953. Olding's (founded in 1935) moved to Hatfield in 1939 and during the Second World War changed from making tractors to making armoured vehicles and fitting tank tracks. Completed vehicles were stored in Hatfield Park before removal to war zones. The company merged with Scottish Land Development to become SLD Olding in 1969 and continued making tractors and agricultural machinery. Jack Olding died in June 1958 having made his name between the wars in the motor trade before diversifying into tractors. The factory was demolished in 1986 when Tesco's, Homebase, and Habitat (later joined by Comet) superstores were built on the site.

134 M. Cook & Son moved from Islington when their new factory in Great Braitch Lane, Hatfield was completed in 1937. Founded by Matilda Cook in 1860 as Cook Cardboard Boxes, it first made corrugated containers in 1923. The largest of the machines at Hatfield at the time of opening was a 245 ft. American one acquired by the Company's Managing Director, H.F. Warbey. By 1950 Cook's Corrugated Cases (as it was then known) had expanded and employed over 400 staff. Its distinctive central tower was very similar to that at Jack Olding's factory, opened nearby in 1939. The works is now owned by Smurfit Corrugated.

135 The Home Office began issuing instructions to chief constables on fire precautions, air raid warnings and the treatment of aliens 10 years before the outbreak of war. During the Munich detente war training was stepped up considerably, especially for special constables who had an important rôle to play in a force that was already 36 under strength before war broke out in September 1939. By June 1943 there were 79 men in the three services. Staff shortages were made up from the Police War Reserve and the Women's Auxiliary Police Corps in addition to the members of the Special Constabulary who did much security work on top of their normal occupations. This photograph of Hatfield special constables in 1938-9 includes Superintendent Col. W.M.L. Escombe, flanked by Inspector Lionel Sherriff (of the grain merchants) and Sergeant Joe Walby (of Walby butchers). Reg Simmons of the eponymous bakery is second from the right of the front row. First on the left in the same row is Eric Tingey, whose father, Edmund Tingey J.P., was responsible for swearing in the constables. The first uniforms issued at this time consisted only of cap, staff, armlet and whistle.

136 St John Ambulance and Air Raid Precautions Wardens outside the Memorial Hall, *c.*1940. (*Back row, left to right*) Geoff Harradine, Tom Clark, Arthur Nash, George Davidson, Sid Mills, Stan Harradine and Mr. Cooper. (*Front row, left to right*) William Halsey, Chief Officer Hugh Jenkins and Len Cull.

137 At about midday on Thursday, 3 October 1940, a lone Junkers 88 German bomber, flying at about 50 ft., flew undetected over de Havilland's, dropping four bombs on the airfield. One bounced into 94 Paint Shop, killing 21 people and wounding 70 others. Ironically, the German pilot, when captured later, was said to have been a de Havilland apprentice during peacetime and to have learned to fly at Hatfield. As local gun emplacements on the airfield and on the hilltops to the west and south opened up, the aircraft was hit and crashed in a field on East End Green Farm, near Cole Green a few miles away. The pilot and his three crew were captured by farmworkers, disarmed and handed to the local Home Guard.

138 A keep fit team from de Havilland's demonstrating in front of a Rapide. All factories had fitness regimes, many inspired, as this one, by Eileen Fowler who promoted a national programme of fitness for women engaged in the war effort.

139 During the Second World War most large factories had their own Local Defence Volunteers or Home Guard Company. One such was B Company, 14th Hertfordshire Battalion based at Jack Oldings Ltd. at Mount Pleasant in 1942 under the command of Capt. J.A. Taylor. At this date few men had uniforms, as direct enrolment into the Home Guard was only just beginning. The nearby de Havilland Aircraft Co. had already raised its own Company of Home Guard in December 1940.

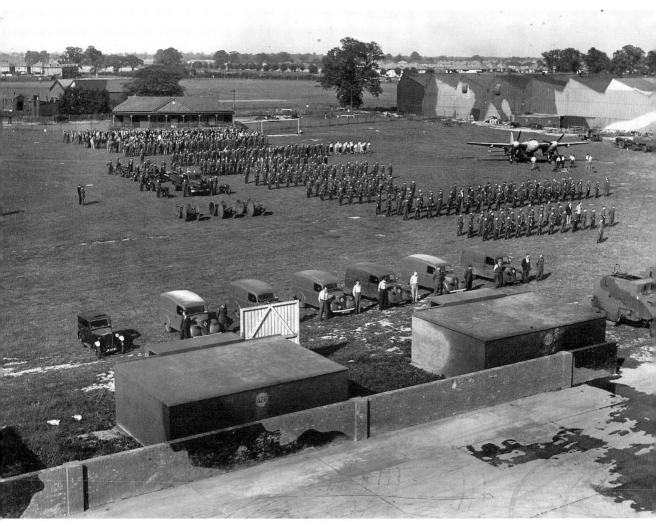

140 Local Home Guard Companies and Royal Observer Corps members parade at de Havilland's in 1942. There were four Companies of 13 Bn Hertfordshire Regiment at the factory, and four others of 14 Bn at Hatfield; Jack Olding's factory; Essendon and Brookmans Park. Two specialist light anti-aircraft troops were also formed specifically to defend de Havilland's. Equipment on display included armoured vehicles, light vans, despatch motorcycles and three-inch Smith guns. Much local Home Guard training took place in Hatfield Park.

141 Early in the morning of 10 October 1944 a flying bomb destroyed St Audrey's School. The older part of the school building, the police cottages across the road and a row of houses known as Primrose Cottages were badly damaged or destroyed. Eight people were killed and 30 seriously injured. There was blast damage to a further 200 buildings, including the Rural District Council offices and the Congregational Church. By the following Monday, St. Audrey's School staff had managed to re-open classes in various buildings in the town. A new building was erected on the old site. Opened in July 1946, it became one of the first County Council controlled schools.

142 Some of the Hatfield Home Guard, with spigot mortars and cases, in Hatfield Park, 1944. The Park was used extensively for Home Guard training, carrying on a long tradition of use by volunteer forces since the 18th century. Local units of 14 Bn Herts HG were under the command of Lt. Col. R.N. Greenwood, M.C. and were considerably better trained and armed by this date. The final stand down also took place in the Park when Lord Cranborne and others addressed the troops. Pictured (*standing from left to right*): Sergeant J.P.B. Clarke and Sergeant Joe Hanlon. (*kneeling from left to right*): Corporal Holmes, Private M. Stokes, Private Bob Pankhurst.

143 (*right*) This photograph, taken in 1946, records some of the de Havilland workers involved in Mosquito production with the last Mosquito bomber built at the Hatfield factory. It was a B35 version and carried the serial number TK656. The very last Hatfield-built 'Wooden Wonder' left the factory in 1949.

144 (*below*) During the Second World War, parts of Hatfield House were released for use as a Convalescent Hospital. Some of the state rooms were filled with iron hospital beds and Lord and Lady Salisbury regularly visited the patients, doctors and nurses. Most of the wounded recovered, but the 21 who died here are commemorated in an official war cemetery near the West Lodge of the House.

145 (*below*) Members of the Hatfield National Fire Service outside the fire station in Batterdale in 1945. Apart from basic fire fighting duties and calls, the volunteers were trained to deal with small incendiary bombs and similar wartime emergencies and to support the regular fire brigade. Fifty-five people died in bombing incidents alone, many more being injured. Note the Women's Land Army poster advertising a dance at the *Stonehouse Hotel* in aid of the 'Red Cross Prisoner of War Fund (Belsen Camp)', accompanied by local businessman Sid Rumbelow's Dance Orchestra.

146 Victory in Europe Party, Hatfield Garden Village, 8 May 1945, at Manor Parade shops.

147　The Women's Land Army hostel in Hollybush Lane, Hatfield Hyde, was run by the Hertfordshire Agricultural Executive Committee. Miss Gladys Flitton (pictured second from left) joined the residents of the hostel on 2 June 1947. Out of the £3 0s. 0d. per week wage, 23s. was deducted for 'living accommodation' and paid to the warden, Mrs. Webster. Miss Flitton (WLA No. 182656) was discharged from the hostel on 21 October 1949, after two years of hard, but enjoyable, work on local farms in the area.

148 The showing of newsreel footage relating to H.M.S. *Amethyst* during the Yangste river incident in November 1949 prompted the manager of the Odeon to ask the Hatfield and District Society of Model Engineers to mount a display in an alcove of the foyer. Interest was heightened by the fact that Jack Day (son of Ken Day, landlord of the newly built *Hopfields* in Birchwood) was serving on the *Amethyst* at this time. The model is that of a battle class destroyer, H.M.S. *Vigo*. It was a joint effort by society members, one of whom was the late Mr. H.J. King of Stanborough.

149 Prefabricated buildings ('prefabs') were introduced after the Second World War to relieve chronic housing shortages. Many remained far longer than first intended. In Hatfield 'prefabs' were erected in large numbers in the field behind the *Wrestlers* public house and in Oxlease. In February 1964 plans were made to demolish all those in Hillfield, Great Heath and Wood Common, those in Flaxland and Little Mead following later. In all 105 aluminium 'prefabs' were removed and flats built on the site. Within two years no 'prefabs' remained and today only in nearby Essendon village can any be seen, near the Mill.

150 The annual inspection of the Hatfield Division of the St John Ambulance Brigade outside St Luke's Church on Sunday, 21 June 1953. There was a railway branch of the St John in Hatfield before the men's branch was established in 1934 and a nursing branch in 1937. They met under the stage of the Public Hall on the Great North Road and at the old Cecil Memorial Hall before moving to their present headquarters at the old Reading Room (next to St Luke's Church), which they shared with the Red Cross until 1994. The inspection was carried out by Commissioner L.R.N. Percey (seated seventh from the right-hand side of the second row). Next to him is the County Superintendent Miss Sparkes and next to her is County President Mrs. McCorquodale, better known as Barbara Cartland, romantic novelist.

151 Aftermath of the gale of the night of 3-4 November 1957 which stripped the roofs off 28 houses and damaged 18 others in South Hatfield. All were of similar construction and were situated on the windward slope of the first rising ground after the extensive plain of the river Colne. The inquiry which followed blamed the architects for the faulty design of the roofs, the clerk of works for inadequate supervision of their installation and the building contractors for not following the architects' instructions. The Hatfield Development Corporation suffered a very heavy financial loss, £67,000, which was not recovered for some years. The metal straps placed over the roofs at the end of each terrace block after the gale are still in place today.

152 Work on the 'Blue Streak' Intermediate Range Ballistic Missile initially began at the Royal Aircraft Establishment at Farnborough in May 1955. Later the project moved to the Hawker Siddeley Dynamics site off Manor Road, Hatfield, where this photograph was taken in October 1961. It was to be the first stage of a multi-stage launch vehicle for an Inter-Continental Ballistic Missile, but after several years of government indecision the project was cancelled in April 1960. 'Blue Streak' was then developed as a first-stage rocket for European satellite launches, but not for long at Hatfield, where the site remained derelict for many years afterwards.

153 'The Breaks' was built in 1930 as a private residence for stockbroker Lionel Edward Janson. Before this he had lived at Great Nast Hyde House. In 1951 it was acquired by the Hatfield Development Corporation, since when it has played an important and continuing rôle as a thriving and successful youth club, with its own warden and management committee. This photograph, taken c.1960, shows the main house and the pre-cast sectional building given by the de Havilland Aircraft Co. in 1958, since when other buildings and facilities have been added.

154 Burleigh School in Wellfield Road was amongst the first of the pioneering 'system built' schools in the town, developed by Hertfordshire County Council. Designed by the Architects Co-partnership as a secondary school with 450 places, it opened for the first time to pupils on Monday 6 September 1954, only to close early because parts of the building were not quite complete! Its first head was Mr. J.E. Kirkham. After a serious fire it was enlarged and parts were rebuilt, and it remained as a school until 1969. Afterwards the buildings were used as a music, teachers' and schools' library service centre as well as being used for community activities like Hatfield Drama. The Burleigh Centre closed in 1993, the buildings were demolished and houses were built on the site in 1994-5.

155 Hatfield Technical College was built by Hertfordshire County Council on a large site at Roe Green presented by Mr. A.S. Butler, then Chairman of de Havillands. It became the Hatfield College of Technology in 1958. Academic standards had reached university standard by the time it was designated Hatfield Polytechnic in 1969. Since 1992 it has been the main Hatfield campus of the University of Hertfordshire.

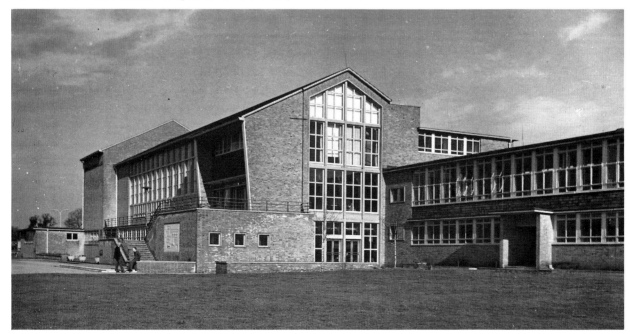

156 Aerial view, looking west, Hatfield New Town Centre under development, September 1958. Cavendish Way, by-passing the new town centre, can be seen to the left of the old St Albans Road. In the lower part of the photograph are the old Cecil Memorial Hall and St Luke's Church and cemetery. At the centre left are the first buildings of Market Square and the Central Arcade. To their right is the north-western corner of White Lion Square. Beyond this are the five Rights of Way connecting St Albans Road with Common Road (now The Common). At the centre top of the photograph is the double row of Gracemead Cottages, built by the Great Northern Railway Company at the turn of the century.

157 White Lion Square is well on the way to completion in this view from the newly-constructed Queensway House, taken in June 1962. In the lower half of the photograph is the mostly 1920s southern side of the St Albans Road. The *White Lion* public house has been demolished and is surrounded on two sides by advertisement hoardings. Immediately behind the new development, on the corner of The Common and Wellfield Road, is the old Labour club building. Ironically, the Conservative Association now has a building on the same site! Also visible is the Wellfield Hospital, the former workhouse, just to the right of the picture's centre.

158 Queensway House and the adjoining public library were opened officially on 19 September 1962 by the Rt. Hon. Sir Keith Joseph M.P. (then Minister of Housing and Local Government). The high-rise flats were designed by Ronald Ward & Partners and built by Bovis and, with Goldings House nearby, have dominated the Hatfield skyline ever since. Its ground floor originally housed small business units, including Polaroid (U.K.) Ltd. and a dental appliance manufacturer. This photograph taken from the Market Place, in 1967, shows the balcony shops and market superintendent's office, demolished and replaced in 1989.

159 Mrs. E.S. Stanyon, one of the first users of Hatfield's new public library on Queensway. Officially opened by Sir Keith Joseph on 19 September 1962, it opened to the public two days later. However, Hatfield's first public lending service was a subscription library founded by Lord Salisbury in 1858. Known as the Hatfield Rural Library, it survived until about 1929. Fines were introduced by 1926 when the library had 151 subscribers. The first county council run service was opened on 20 April 1925 by Mrs. E.I. Speaight at the Girls' School, London Road (open Monday evenings only). Stock was stored in wooden boxes and changed periodically. From 1928 it moved to the Public Hall, Great North Road (Hon. Librarian, Mrs. L.C. Whitby), opening Tuesday evenings and Saturday afternoons. In 1936 the library moved to a large room in the Congregational Church Hall, St Albans Road, but still operated largely out of book boxes, as there were no shelves. Finally, it moved to a wooden hut behind the Rural District Council offices almost opposite in 1954, where it remained until the first purpose built public library was completed eight years later.

160 Hatfield Town Centre, June 1970. Just visible on the right-hand side is the water feature by local artist, David Butler.

161 Gracemead Cottages, St Albans Road, were built by the Great Northern Railway for company employees, *c.*1901. They were better built than the mid-19th-century housing of Newtown. They were of brick with tiled roofs and sash windows, three rooms upstairs and two down, a small back-yard with a closet (complete with flush lavatory). On the right-hand side is the sign of the *Boar and Castle* beer house which stood between the Fourth and Fifth Rights of Way. In its last years it was owned by Whitbread, who closed the pub in 1964.

162 The Common, looking west towards Galleycroft House, which was demolished to make room for the Hatfield swimming pool, completed in 1966. On the right-hand side is the parade of shops and the cinema, established in 1935, renamed the Odeon from 1946 to 1967, now the Chequers Bingo Club.

163 Hatfield swimming pool was opened by the 6th Marquess of Exeter, himself a former Olympic athlete and Vice President of the International Olympic Committee 1954-66, on 30 September 1966. Designed by W.W. Chapman and H.G. Coulter for the architects Woodroffe, Buchanan & Coulter, its most notable feature was its lightweight hyperbolic paraboloid shell roof made by Caxton Reinforced Concrete of London. It was one of the first and largest roofs of its kind in Europe. Inside was a main pool 110 ft. long, of variable depth and built to ASA standards, plus a beginners' or learners' pool with spectators' gallery above. The pool was closed in November 1989 for major reconstruction and refurbishment, and reopened as the Hatfield Swim Centre in April 1991. It was all a long way from Hatfield's earlier 'pool' created in the river Lea at Mill Green in the 1920s.

164 Aerial view of the western end of the New Town centre, showing the Woolco store built across the line of the old St Albans Road which opened in autumn 1972. One of the first hypermarkets built in Britain, it was taken over by Gateway in 1987 and by Asda three years later.

165 St John's Church in South Hatfield stands at the highest point in the town. The foundation stone was laid by Princess Alexandra on 14 June 1958 and the completed building was consecrated by the Bishop of St Albans on 26 March 1960. The church and adjoining priest's house were designed by Messrs. Lionel Brett, Boyd and Bosanquet; a campanile was planned but never built. The steeply pitched roof, the extensive use of timber inside and the small rectangles of glass in the east wall combine to create a warmth and lightness in the interior. In recent years, the cost of heat loss in the large interior open roof space has proved a financial and practical problem.

166 The St Etheldreda's bellringers, photographed in 1972. From *left to right*, Eileen Tipping, John Ford, Alison Thomas, Colin Rees, Michael Peers, Elizabeth Saunders, Sue Rees, Ted Chambers, John Boyce, Nicholas Hughes, Stan Huckle, Russell Brown, Paula Healing, David Kemp, and Bob Cochrane. Bellringing at the church has a long and distinguished past, beginning with the Hatfield College Youths in the late 18th century. The tower contains 10 bells, seven made by John Briant of Hertford in 1786, two by Mears & Stainbank of London in 1929, and one by Thomas Mears in 1841.

167 Hatfield's new Roman Catholic church, Marychurch, nearing completion in 1970. Its modern design, adjacent to older buildings, caused some controversy at the time. Designed by Mathers, Thomas & Associates, its narrow windows, filled with coloured glass designed and made by Dom. Charles Norris and Paulinus Angold of Buckfast Abbey, enhances the striking interior. The central altar was made by Arthur Wiseman of Hatfield. The church seats about 450 people comfortably. To its left the former church (now a hall) and seminary of 1930.

168 Goldings House, a high-rise block designed for young single people, was opened on 29 May 1968 by Sir Henry Wells, Chairman, Commission for the New Towns. The architects were Woodroffe, Buchanan & Coulter. The 14-storey block contains 72 flats and 6 maisonettes. Rents were originally between £16 and £24 10s. per month excluding rates.

169 Firs Close, designed by architects Richard Sheppard and Partners, 1969.

170 The old militia cottages in Salisbury Square, April 1972 during demolition, viewed from the top of 'Jacob's Ladder', and looking towards the new railway bridge in French Horn Lane. The white building, centre right in the distance, is one of the four signal boxes once sited near Hatfield station.

171 The old and new railway bridges in French Horn Lane, July 1970. To the left (just out of the picture) once stood the London Road School and the Wesleyan Chapel (opened in 1889), and beyond the bridge on the same side the Hatfield gas works and Glebe Cottages (some of which still remain). On the right the site of Batterdale and just out of the photograph Marychurch is under construction.

172 Batterdale House, better known as The Colonel's House, dated from the late 17th century, being one of the few houses of this period to survive in the town. Priory House was another. Owned originally by Searancke's the brewers, it passed by marriage to Samuel Hare, maltster, in c.1690, remaining in his family until 1806. It was bought by Lord Salisbury a year later. Its name of The Colonel's House appears to date from later that century when Harts Militia were based in Hatfield. However, it was lived in mainly by the Quartermaster Sergeants and their families, not by militia officers. Despite its historical importance, the house did not escape the bulldozer and was demolished in the 1970s.

173 A fine view of a de Havilland 125 business jet aircraft leaving the factory in 1978. Below can be seen the original de Havilland offices, factory buildings and airfield of the 1930s. Opposite them are two of the original four blocks of once luxury apartments, built in the mid-1930s and named Rodney, Altham, Haddon and Cumberland Courts (demolished in 1979), and behind them Lemsford Road, Stockbreach Road and Close, part of the Burleigh School site; and, in the left foreground, part of the Common.

174 Hatfield Concert Band was some five years old when this photograph was taken in 1984. Founded by local resident George A. Hill, the band held its first rehearsal at Onslow School on 11 September 1979. Sponsorship initially was received from Hatfield Laundry. The band's first musical director was John Collinge and its first public performance was given at the Forum Theatre in Hatfield on 25 March 1980. Since then, the H.C.B. has given concerts at many local and other venues, including Hatfield's twin town of Zieriksee in Holland, and once appeared regularly at British Aerospace open days. In 1984 the band issued its first full-length cassette. A specially composed tribute entitled Jetset 81 was written by John Collinge to commemorate the first flight of the BAe 146.

175 Ashley Court in Wellfield Road was opened by David Evans, M.P. for Welwyn Hatfield Constituency (*right above*), on 1 September 1987. The 33 flats for the elderly were built by the Shaftesbury Society. Fourteen bungalows were added later. The complex is one of many in the area built by the county or district council, or privately, since the 1960s. The building stands on the site of the Hatfield Laundry founded 1931, demolished in 1986. The laundry began in business after the First World War as the Newtown Hand Laundry, then Woolven's Laundry before adopting its last name.

176 Penny Matthews (née Simmons), and Ruth Coles (née Simmons), May 1988 during the 150th anniversary year of Simmons the Bakers. The firm has its origins in the bakery founded by Maria Hulks at Roe Green in the 1830s. The Simmons family were cousins of the Hulks. In the 1930s Reginald C. Simmons of Roe Green and H. Hill & Son of Fore Street and Great North Road went into partnership as Hill & Simmons Ltd. The business was much expanded by Reginald Simmons from the 1950s and now has a catering arm and 20 branches in Hertfordshire.

177 The Galleria is an American-style shopping development, with multiplex cinema and fast-food outlets, built on top of Hatfield Tunnel. Conceived as a centre for luxury shopping, it opened in 1991 as the economy nosedived into recession. A year later, the operating company went into receivership. In October 1993 Waxy Management purchased the complex. They have since re-launched it as a centre for 'value' shopping with American retailers T.K. Maxx as flagship store. The nine-screen cinema has been a tremendous success and is the busiest multiplex in the south-east.

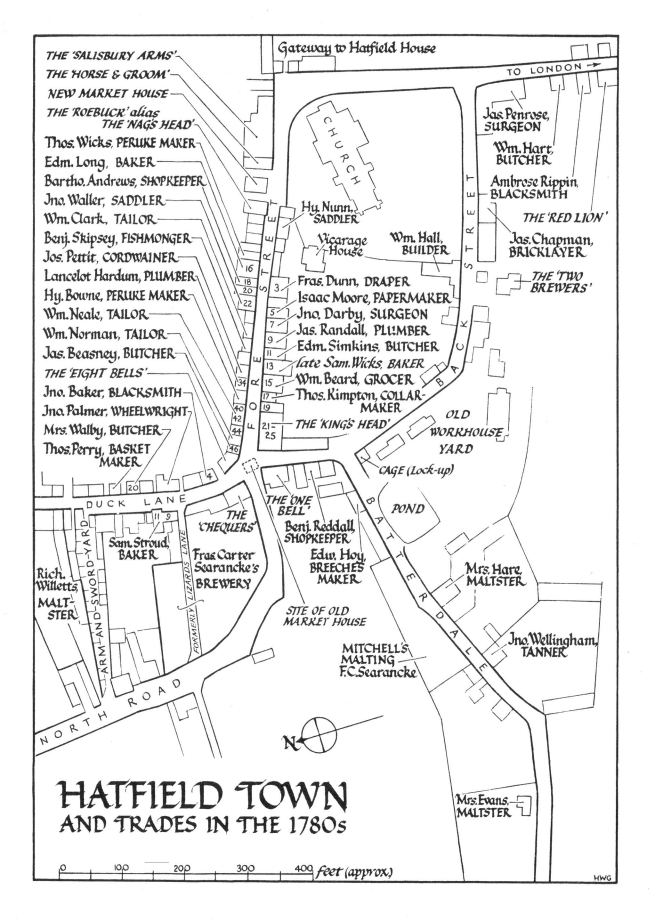

Gateway to Hatfield House

TO LONDON →

THE 'SALISBURY ARMS'
THE 'HORSE & GROOM'
NEW MARKET HOUSE
THE 'ROEBUCK' alias
          THE 'NAGS HEAD'
Thos. Wicks, PERUKE MAKER
Edm. Long, BAKER
Bartho. Andrews, SHOPKEEPER
Jno. Waller, SADDLER
Wm. Clark, TAILOR
Benj. Skipsey, FISHMONGER
Jos. Pettit, CORDWAINER
Lancelot Hardum, PLUMBER
Hy. Bowne, PERUKE MAKER
Wm. Neale, TAILOR
Wm. Norman, TAILOR
Jas. Beasney, BUTCHER
THE 'EIGHT BELLS'
Jno. Baker, BLACKSMITH
Jno. Palmer, WHEELWRIGHT
Mrs. Walby, BUTCHER
Thos. Perry, BASKET
          MAKER

CHURCH

Jas. Penrose, SURGEON
Wm. Hart, BUTCHER
Ambrose Rippin, BLACKSMITH
THE 'RED LION'
Jas. Chapman, BRICKLAYER
THE 'TWO BREWERS'

Hy. Nunn, SADDLER
Vicarage House
Wm. Hall, BUILDER

FORE STREET

BACK STREET

16
18
20
22
3
Fras. Dunn, DRAPER
5   Isaac Moore, PAPERMAKER
7   Jno. Darby, SURGEON
9   Jas. Randall, PLUMBER
11 Edm. Simkins, BUTCHER
13 late Sam. Wicks, BAKER
34 15 Wm. Beard, GROCER
17 Thos. Kimpton, COLLAR-
40   MAKER
42 19
44 21   THE 'KING'S HEAD'
46 25

OLD WORKHOUSE YARD

CAGE (Lock-up)

4
20

DUCK LANE

11 9
Sam. Stroud, BAKER

THE 'CHEQUERS'
Fras. Carter Searancke's BREWERY

ARMAND-SWORD-YARD

FORMERLY LIZARDS LANE

THE 'ONE BELL'
Benj. Reddall, SHOPKEEPER
Edw. Hoy, BREECHES MAKER

POND

Rich. Willetts, MALT-STER

SITE OF OLD MARKET HOUSE

MITCHELL'S MALTING
F.C. Searancke

Mrs. Hare, MALTSTER

Jno. Wellingham, TANNER

BATTERDALE

NORTH ROAD

N

Mrs. Evans, MALTSTER

HATFIELD TOWN
AND TRADES IN THE 1780s

0   100   200   300   400 feet (approx.)

HWG